A MI

An A.

C. S. Lewis

BOOKS BY C. S. LEWIS

A MIND AWAKE
An Anthology of
C. S. Lewis

❧❧❧❧❧❧❧❧❧❧❧❧❧❧❧❧❧❧❧❧❧❧❧❧❧

EDITED BY

Clyde S. Kilby

A Harvest Book
Harcourt Brace & Company
San Diego   New York   London

Excerpts from the following are reprinted by permission of Macmillan Publishing Co., Inc. All rights reserved. *The Screwtape Letters, The Problem of Pain, Mere Christianity, The Abolition of Man, The Great Divorce, Miracles, The Weight of Glory,* copyright Macmillan Publishing Co., Inc. 1943, 1944, 1945, 1946, 1947, 1949; *The Lion, the Witch and the Wardrobe, Prince Caspian, The Voyage of the* Dawn Treader, *The Silver Chair, The Horse and His Boy,* copyright Arthur Owen Barfield, Alfred Cecil Harwood, and Walter Hooper, trustees of the Estate of C. S. Lewis, 1950, 1951, 1952, 1953, 1954; *Out of the Silent Planet, Perelandra, That Hideous Strength, The Magician's Nephew, The Last Battle,* copyright C. S. Lewis 1944, 1945 © C. S. Lewis 1955, 1956; "Introduction" by C. S. Lewis to *Letters to Young Churches,* by J. B. Phillips, copyright J. B. Phillips 1947.

Library of Congress Cataloging-in-Publication Data
Lewis, Clive Staples, 1898–1963.
A mind awake.
(A Harvest book)
1. Theology—Collected works—20th century.
I. Kilby, Clyde S. II. Title.
[BT15.L48 1980] 230 80-14133
ISBN 0-15-659772-1

Printed in the United States of America

First Harvest edition 1980

F G H I J

CONTENTS

PREFACE

Clive Staples Lewis was born in Belfast on 29 November 1898. Before he was ten his mother had started him in French, Latin and the reading of fiction. After preparatory study in Irish and English schools, he attended Malvern College in England for one year and then studied for Oxford under W. T. Kirkpatrick at Great Bookham in Surrey. By this time—he was sixteen—he had become an inveterate reader, fallen in love with romantic story and northern myth, been engulfed by the haunting mystery of Joy, developed into an habitual walker, learned to revel in the glory of the English countryside, and turned atheist. Oddly, however, it was the rigorous dialectic taught by Kirkpatrick, himself an atheist, which in due course brought Lewis to Christianity.

On his nineteenth birthday Lewis, a second lieutenant in the Somerset Light Infantry, arrived in the front-line trenches of France, where he was wounded in action. Before enlisting he had attended University College, Oxford, and after the war he returned. In 1920 he took a First Honour in Moderations, in 1922 a First in Greats, and in 1923 a First in English, also the Chancellor's Prize for an English Essay. In October 1924 he became a lecturer at University College, and in 1925 took up his work as Fellow at Magdalen. Four years later the most important event of his life occurred. He was converted to Christianity. He remained at Magdalen until 1954 when he was elected to the Chair of Medieval and Renaissance English at Magdalene College, Cambridge, a post he held until a few weeks before his death on 22 November 1963.

Lewis was among the great teachers of his generation. He had both a powerful, discriminating mind and brilliance of language. He was lightning quick in noting any logical flaw in even a casual remark. In the presentation of an abstruse idea in criticism or in theology, he had a natural tendency toward analogy and metaphor. Once after an involved debate on Christianity and culture he said, 'If we could thrash the problem out on the neutral ground of clean and dirty fingers, we might return to the battlefield of literature with new lights.' He liked his ideas to fit the truth as snugly as old slippers fit the feet, and he dropped many of his most provocative thoughts as lightly as a feather.

A visitor to the Socratic Society of Oxford gives a lively account of Lewis. He wore 'an old battered tweed sports coat . . . well-worn corduroy trousers, a patterned, well-washed shirt with a nondescript antique type tie. He was ruddy of complexion, radiating health, of substantial girth all over, and his eyes sparkled with mirth'. The subject for the evening was the meaning of history and a professor of history buried his nose in a dull paper and read endlessly while the audience listened sleepily. When it came Lewis's turn to speak, there was immediate attention. 'He was exciting. . . . Vivid images and portraits just tumbled out of him. He had no notes and spoke spontaneously with charm and lilt.' His lectures were crowded and students left them with the sense of genuine acquisition.

It was not, however, as lecturer to a few hundred students or private associations but as writer to thousands that Lewis is best known. His brother tells us that before Lewis was thirteen he had produced a complete novel. His published works run to more than forty volumes, including poetry, short stories, novels, children's stories, allegory, letters, literary criticism, studies in philology and learned works on medieval and renaissance literature. Both as scholar and as creative writer he was praised, and indeed these two qualities join in whatever mode he used. Immense knowledge, logic and imagination joined in Lewis to make him one of the finest Christian apologists of our time.

Occasionally over-assertive and unduly combative in conversation, Lewis actually belonged to the greatly good men of all time. Like Dr Samuel Johnson, though dialectically formidable and capable of annihilating an opponent, Lewis was yet nobly humble of heart. He risked and in some measure, especially among his colleagues at Oxford and Cambridge, damaged his scholarly reputation by writing books that warmly and wittily defended orthodox Christianity. Again like Johnson, Lewis was perfectly at home among Greek and Latin texts and languages generally, but he contrasted with the Great Cham in the far-flung strength and grace of his imagination.

The paradoxes are as much accentuated in Lewis's personal as in his scholarly life. A man of phenomenal memory, his mind was all but a blank when it came to making up a list of his own books and articles. Hating letter writing as the chief burden of his life, he nevertheless spent long hours answering, mostly in his own hand, correspondents around the world. A lover of solitude or else his small circle of intimates, he made even casual visitors to his rooms in the university feel leisurely at home. Completely erudite in the philosophical highlands, he was at the same time a man of simplest affections and in whom 'the element of play was never far away', as his delightful stories for children prove, and this despite the fact that he disliked the society of small children. So much a lover of nature that on one occasion at least he stood outside to enjoy the scene while dictating to his secretary through the open window, Lewis nevertheless spent his life as a sedentary scholar. By his own admission awkward in his social affairs, he acted on his conviction of Christian duty to sit at the bedside of the sick and personally serve the poor. He gave away two-thirds of his income and would have given more except for income taxes. Though severely wounded on the western front in World War I, he made light of his military service. Believing the modern world to be quite literally in a hellish tailspin, he was nevertheless a man of unceasing personal cheerfulness. A man of massive intellect, he was at the same time a true mystic in the sense of believing absolutely in God.

Actually Lewis is paradoxical on a small view, not much so on a large. The world is so little used to seeing a *believer* that it is easy to see him as an oddity. He had so little confidence in the works of men that he took his own books with several grains of salt and actually forgot some of their titles. Though he might easily have justified himself as serving God by writing books which made profound spiritual impressions, he nevertheless believed that a Christian needed to make personal contacts for God. Lover of nature, he always remembered that nature's beauty 'withers when we try to make it an absolute' In a word, he was a man with a clear and operating hierarchy and hence suffered a minimum from the present ubiquitous practice of making man the real measure of things. He once described himself as a 'converted pagan living among apostate Puritans' and 'a man who had taken as long to' acquire inhibitions as others have needed to get rid of them. He enjoyed, perhaps too much, calling himself an Old Western Man and taking potshots at nearly everything modern. Yet beneath his lance breaking there was a world of spiritual actualities. For instance, as few today, Lewis saw and feared the sinuosity of pride, calling it 'the essential vice, the utmost evil . . . the complete anti-God state of mind'. He regarded such spiritual sins as far more vicious than our overt ones.

He was able to find deep satisfaction in things ordinarily taken for granted—a blade of grass, sunlight falling on a tree, the ride from the university on the public bus and the walk down Kiln Lane to his beloved home ('I love monotony,' he once said), fairy stories, cheerfulness, humility, courtesy even to dogs and cats, the true brotherhood of man and also the unique individual (his housekeeper told me that he would talk at length with her and claimed he learned much from her), and of life itself as a constant miracle.

He was not unlike Aslan, his own Christ-symbol in the Narnia stories. Aslan was a loving but never a tame lion and did not hesitate to bowl the children over or put a substantial scratch on them to turn them away from a worse danger ahead. Lewis had the gift of loving his generation and tempering his scratches to his clear view of man's real needs rather than the shoddy ones to which we are ordinarily addicted. Someone objected to Lewis's trying to solve such great problems as pain and miracles in a relatively small book. But he believed that such problems had at least essential answers and set out like a hound on the scent of a fox to find them. He liked answers better than questions.

Lewis's Christian books are remarkably 'of a piece'. In *The Christian World of C. S. Lewis* I have mentioned some of his main themes—his wish to uphold the reality and utter truthfulness of orthodox Christianity his assurance that all men are destined to eternal life either in heaven or in hell and his belief that momentarily they are preparing themselves for one place or the other, his belief that God is to be obeyed explicitly, his conviction of a devilish fallacy at the centre of much modern thought, that the elevation of self over God is perhaps man's most persistent temptation, and his often mentioned belief that many world myths are shadows of the light of God brooding over man.

Although in selecting the entries for this anthology I paid no attention to themes, their appearance was not surprising, as chapter titles and sub-headings indicate. Lewis's constant allusions to God's gift of selfhood and the dire dangers of its abuse are well represented. As might be expected, there is much about contemporary times. Perhaps the best evidence of all of Lewis's basic aim in his Christian works is the large chapter on 'Christianity and the Church' and especially the portion of it given to the practice of a holy life. Though one section is marked 'Hierarchy', the whole volume might not inappropriately be called by that title. All other things are seen in the light and by the standard of the great 'I Am' and take their values from that fact. For a writer who always described

himself as no theologian, there is a great deal on the Trinity.
One fact which will not surprise readers of the children's books
is the frequency of entries concerning salvation. Also the idea
that 'Aslan is not a tame lion' is hammered home not only
there but in the majority of Lewis's Christian works.

Concerning a distinguished colleague of his, Lewis said, 'Of
such a man's mind the least gleanings are venerable.' I suppose
this is the assumption on which anthologies are generally produced. One wishes to preserve in a single place the essential
wisdom of the man. At the same time it would be a mistake to
substitute such a collection, valuable as it is, for the works
proper. Shakespeare anthologized is something quite different
from Shakespeare dramatized. To appreciate an anthology ade-
quately, one needs to have walked along the level floor of the
author's mind, or, to change the figure, to have examined not
simply the diamond in the ring but the ring, the hand, and indeed the person wearing it. Good writing always pleases both
by the excellence of its parts and the perfection of the whole.
Here we have the parts, and it is hoped that they may make the
reader turn, or turn again, to the whole body of Lewis's works.

Because this is primarily a collection of Lewis's remarks on
Christian themes it omits most of his comments, pungent as
many of them are, on literature, criticism and other purely
scholarly subjects. Nevertheless, it was one of the distinguish-
ing aspects of Lewis's thought that his Christian books were
marked by a profound logic ('brevity comparable to St Paul's'
and argument 'distilled to the unanswerable', said the New
York *Times* of one book of his), and his scholarly works never
ignored the Christian philosophy at the base of his thought.
To him the world was a unity with God as its sovereign creator and unceasing ruler. For this reason it will be noticed that
every one of his books, together with most of his uncollected
essays and articles and even a few still manuscript remarks, are
included in this volume.

Expository books lend themselves better to quotation than do poetry and fiction. Nearly three-fourths of the material in Lewis's anthology of George MacDonald is taken from expository volumes by that writer. Some of Lewis's own expository books, such as *The Problem of Pain* and *Miracles*, are so rich that it is difficult to make proper selections from them. *Mere Christianity*, though rewarding in ideas, is often lacking in the shapeliness of expression that an anthology demands, perhaps because it was originally spoken into the microphones of the BBC. Oddly, I find relatively little that I judge suitable for the anthology in his novel *Out of the Silent Planet*, but in the companion novel *Perelandra*, once the 'temptation' scenes begin, there is something on almost every page that might be used. I have found it especially hard to choose passages from Lewis's poetry, not because it is not rich in content and style but because each poem is so completely a unity that parts are usually not detachable.

Worthy as it might be, my aim has not been to compile a book of what Lewis believed. For instance, he held that pacifists are wrong and he steadfastly refused to be classified as High, Low or Broad Church, but such opinions are omitted. Although passages on such subjects as the inspiration of the Bible are included, there is no systematic 'covering' of the subject. An anthology is no place for answers to criticisms or fine-pointed arguments. To be sure, on every page one will discover Lewis's spiritual convictions, but never as systematic theology. Nor is this volume intended primarily as 'spiritual uplift' or sermonic exhortation to lead men to Christ or Christians to a closer walk with God. Though one could wish that the book might often have these effects, it is nevertheless of another sort.

Neither have I attempted to wedge into the anthology interesting personal aspects of Lewis. Where is there a more picturesque biographical sketch than Lewis's account, in *Surprised by Joy* and the *Letters*, of his father? Where clearer detail of the

logic which led him to God? Where a better account of the war
years at Oxford? But an anthology is not the place for such
things.

Again, in certain instances passages were not amenable to
the length I regarded best. The vivid accounts, for instance, in
The Great Divorce, of the conversion of the lustful man and
of the tragedian striking poses against heavenly reason are
examples of excellent things which had to be passed over.
Many passages in *The Pilgrim's Regress* presented the same
difficulty, e.g. the Freudian jailer who persuaded the prisoners
to believe that their own viscera were the only true reality.

But I should say what I *have* sought to include. First, I have
followed the tradition of 'wit and wisdom' by seeking entries
containing the pungent and provocative idea. Secondly, and
again in the tradition of anthologies, I have chosen self-
contained remarks, i.e. ones requiring no editorial explanation or comment. Thirdly, it need hardly be mentioned that
entries should be in the best style. Often in one way or another
they embody a figure of speech. Fourthly, I have desired to
include not simply aphoristic remarks as such but rather ideas
shaped and coloured by the particular bias of Lewis's mind.
It is a *Lewis* anthology.

It is obvious that no two people endeavouring to select the
best from a man's works will always choose identical passages,
and the richer the content of those works the less likelihood of
total agreement. Concerning the making of anthologies Lewis
himself once remarked, 'No man ever agrees with another
man's choice, and to disagree is one of the pleasures of using an
anthology.' Nothing more can be said than that here you have
my own choices based on thirty-odd years of reading and re-
reading Lewis.

Speaking of an anthology which he reviewed, Lewis said,
'If a second edition is called for I hope the editor will tell us
where, in the works of the author, each passage is to be found;
otherwise one of the chief uses of an anthology—that of direct-

ing us to the originals—is frustrated.' Since I heartily agree, I have followed this principle. Yet because there are several editions of most of Lewis's books, I have thought it wise to refer to general units, such as chapters and sections, rather than to specific pages, and this even in cases where presently only one edition is available. In cases where an essay originally appeared in a periodical and was later incorporated in a book, I have, for the convenience of readers, referred to the book. But the acknowledgements below make known the publisher's and my gratitude to the original sources.

Where *Letters* is given as a source the reference is to *Letters of C. S. Lewis*; whereas *Letters to Malcolm* refers to that book.

I have mentioned the frequent use of Lewis's fiction. But I must remind anyone who has had the misfortune not to have read *The Screwtape Letters* that the point of view there is upside down and the 'Enemy' is God.

My first thanks are due the Class of 1963 of Wheaton College, U.S.A., whose financial grant made possible a year's leave of absence from my teaching for the preparation of this anthology and work on other projects.

I express my deep appreciation to the Executors of the Estate of C. S. Lewis for their encouragement in the preparation of this book.

I am grateful to Dr Corbin Carnell, Mr Jocelyn Gibb, the Reverend Walter Hooper and Dr Owen Barfield for criticisms of the manuscript. To the latter two I am indebted for numerous other favours. I take this occasion to mention in particular Mr Hooper's indispensable bibliography which any Lewis student must keep close at hand. My thanks are also due to Miss Agnes Horness and to my wife, Martha, for valuable assistance. It is also my great pleasure to acknowledge the friendship and encouragement of Major W. H. Lewis.

The publisher and I also express our gratitude for permission to use excerpts from the following works by C. S. Lewis:

The Athlone Press for 'The Literary Impact of the Authorised Version' (ch. 2, *They Asked for a Paper*).

The Bristol Diocesan Gazette for 'The Trouble with "X" '.

Cambridge University Press for *De Descriptione Temporum* (ch. 1, *They Asked for a Paper*), *The Discarded Image*, *An Experiment in Criticism*, *Studies in Medieval and Renaissance Literature* and *Studies in Words*.

Church of the Covenant, United Church of Christ, for *Encounter with Light*.

Church Times for two letters by Lewis.

The Clarendon Press, Oxford, for *The Allegory of Love*, *English Literature in the Sixteenth Century* and Lewis's review of *The Oxford Book of Christian Verse* from the 1941 volume of the *Review of English Studies*.

The Coventry Evening Telegraph for 'Who Was Right— Dream Lecturer or Real Lecturer?'

Decision for 'I Was Decided Upon' and 'Heaven, Earth and Outer Space'.

William B. Eerdmans Publishing Company for *Christian Reflections*, a letter in Clyde S. Kilby's *The Christian World of C. S. Lewis* and also several items listed as unpublished letters which are now included in *Letters to an American Lady*.

Essays in Criticism for 'A Note on Jane Austen'.

Executors of Lewis's Estate and Geoffrey Bles for *The Pilgrim's Regress*, *They Asked for a Paper*, *Transpositions and Other Addresses* (Amer. ed., *The Weight of Glory*, pub. by The Macmillan Company), 'A Christian Reply to Professor Price' from the *Phoenix Quarterly*, *A Preface to 'Paradise Lost'* and the introduction to *The Incarnation of the Word of God* by St Athanasius.

Mr W. G. Gardiner and Mr J. S. A. Ensor and the Electric and Musical Industries Christian Fellowship of Hayes, Middlesex, for *Answers to Questions on Christianity*.

Harcourt, Brace & World, Inc. for *The Four Loves, Letters of C. S. Lewis, Letters to Malcolm: Chiefly on Prayer, Of Other Worlds, Poems, Reflections on the Psalms, Rehabilitations and Other Essays, Surprised by Joy, Till We Have Faces* and *The World's Last Night.*

Harper & Row, Publishers, Inc. for the preface to D. E. Harding's *Hierarchy of Heaven and Earth.*

William Heinemann Ltd for *Spirits in Bondage.*

David Higham Associates, Ltd for *Arthurian Torso,* a joint work by Charles Williams and C. S. Lewis.

Hodder and Stoughton Limited for a part of Lewis's foreword to Joy Davidman's *Smoke on the Mountain.*

Lumen Vitae for 'Difficulties in Presenting the Christian Faith to Modern Unbelievers'.

The Macmillan Company for *The Abolition of Man, The Great Divorce, The Horse and His Boy, The Last Battle, The Lion, the Witch and the Wardrobe, The Magician's Nephew, Mere Christianity, Miracles, Out of the Silent Planet, Perelandra, Prince Caspian, The Problem of Pain, The Screwtape Letters, The Silver Chair, That Hideous Strength, The Voyage of the 'Dawn Treader,' The Weight of Glory* and the introduction to *Letters to Young Churches* by J. B. Phillips.

Mother Mary Martin and the Medical Missionaries of Mary for 'Some Thoughts', in *The First Decade: Ten Years' Work of the Medical Missionaries of Mary.*

Melbourne University Law Review (formerly *Res Judicatae*) for 'The Humanitarian Theory of Punishment'.

The New England Anti-Vivisection Society for *Vivisection.*

The Observer for 'Must Our Image of God Go?'

Oxford University Press for *The Personal Heresy* and for an excerpt from R. S. Wright's *Asking Them Questions.*

Punch for 'Revival or Decay?'

St James' Magazine for 'Scraps'.

The Seabury Press, Inc. for *A Grief Observed.*

The Society for Promoting Christian Knowledge for an

excerpt from Lewis's review of Dorothy Sayers's *The Mind of the Maker* (*Theology*, October 1941).

The Socratic Society of Oxford for 'Is Theism Important? A Reply', 'Is Theology Poetry?' (ch. 9, *They Asked for a Paper*) and 'Religion without Dogma', from *The Socratic Digest*.

The Spectator for 'Equality', 'Evil and God', 'Private Bates' and 'Prudery and Philology'.

Student Christian Movement in Schools and the SCM Press Ltd for *Man or Rabbit?*

Time and Tide for 'Notes on the Way' (issues of 17 August 1940, 27 June 1942, 29 April 1944, 1 June 1946, 9 November 1946 and 14 August 1948) and for 'Delinquents in the Snow', 'Haggard Rides Again' and 'Hedonics'.

World Dominion for 'Myth Became Fact'.

Additionally, I should like to thank the following for permission to use material:

The Bodley Head Ltd. for *The Last Battle*, *The Magician's Nephew*, *Out of the Silent Planet*, *Perelandra* and *That Hideous Strength*.

Executors of C. S. Lewis and Geoffrey Bles Ltd. for *The Abolition of Man*, *The Four Loves*, *The Great Divorce*, *The Horse and His Boy*, *Letters of C. S. Lewis*, *Letters to Malcolm: Chiefly on Prayer*, *The Lion, the Witch and the Wardrobe*, *Mere Christianity*, *Miracles*, *Of Other Worlds*, *Poems*, *Prince Caspian*, *The Problem of Pain*, *Reflections on the Psalms*, *The Screwtape Letters*, *The Silver Chair*, *Surprised by Joy*, *Till We Have Faces*, *The Voyage of the 'Dawn Treader'* and the introduction to *Letters to Young Churches* by J. B. Phillips.

Executors of C. S. Lewis and J. M. Dent & Sons Ltd. for *Dymer*.

I

THE NATURE OF MAN

1. MAN IN GOD'S IMAGE

Of each creature we can say, 'This also is Thou: neither is this Thou.'

Simple faith leaps to this with astonishing ease. I once talked to a continental pastor who had seen Hitler, and had, by all human standards, good cause to hate him. 'What did he look like?' I asked. 'Like all men,' he replied. 'That is, like Christ.'

Letters to Malcolm, ch. 14

No good work is done anywhere without aid from the Father of Lights.

Reflections on the Psalms, ch. 11

'. . . the eternal mood
Blowing the eternal theme through men that pass.'

Dymer, canto 8, st. 10

God is present in each thing but not necessarily in the same mode; not in a man as in the consecrated bread and wine, nor in a bad man as in a good one, nor in a beast as in a man, nor in a tree as in a beast, nor in inanimate matter as in a tree. I take it there is a paradox here. The higher the creature, the more, and also the less, God is in it; the more present by grace, and the less present (by a sort of abdication) as mere power. By grace He gives the higher creatures power to will His will ('and wield their little tridents'): the lower ones simply execute it automatically.

Letters to Malcolm, ch. 14

I have said that he was almost wholly logical; but not quite. He had been a Presbyterian and was now an Atheist. He spent Sunday, as he spent most of his time on week-days, working in his garden. But one curious trait from his Presbyterian youth survived. He always, on Sundays, gardened in a different, and slightly more respectable, suit. An Ulster Scot may come to disbelieve in God, but not to wear his weekday clothes on the Sabbath.

Surprised by Joy, ch. 9

'Creation' as applied to human authorship seems to me to be an entirely misleading term. We re-arrange elements He has provided. There is not a vestige of real creativity *de novo* in us. Try to imagine a new primary colour, a third sex, a fourth dimension, or even a monster which does not consist of bits of existing animals stuck together. Nothing happens. And that surely is why our works never mean to others quite what we intended; because we are re-combining elements made by Him and already containing *His* meanings. Because of those divine meanings in our materials it is impossible that we should ever know the whole meaning of our own works, and the meaning we never intended may be the best and truest one. Writing a book is much less like creation than it is like planting a garden or begetting a child; in all three cases we are only entering as *one* cause into a causal stream which works, so to speak, in its own way. I would not wish it to be otherwise. If one could *really* create in the strict sense, would not one find that one had created a sort of Hell?

Letters (20 February 1943)

The deeper the level within ourselves from which our prayer, or any other act, wells up, the more it is His, but not at all the less ours. Rather, most ours when most His. Arnold speaks of us as 'enisled' from one another in 'the sea of life'. But we can't be similarly 'enisled' from God. To be discontinuous from God as I am discontinuous from you would be annihilation.

Letters to Malcolm, ch. 13

2. FALLEN MAN

'You come of the Lord Adam and the Lady Eve,' said Aslan. 'And that is both honour enough to erect the head of the poorest beggar, and shame enough to bow the shoulders of the greatest emperor in earth.'

Prince Caspian, ch. 15

Non-Christians seem to think that the Incarnation implies some particular merit or excellence in humanity. But of course it implies just the reverse: a particular demerit and depravity. No creature that deserved Redemption would need to be redeemed. They that are whole need not the physician. Christ died for men precisely because men are *not* worth dying for; to make them worth it.

The World's Last Night, ch. 6

Surely what a man does when he is taken off his guard is the best evidence for what sort of man he is? . . . If there are rats in a cellar you are most likely to see them if you go in very suddenly. But the suddenness does not create the rats: it only prevents them from hiding. In the same way the suddenness of the provocation does not make me an ill-tempered man: it only shows me what an ill-tempered man I am.

Mere Christianity, bk 4, ch. 7

'Nothing is yet in its true form.'

Till We Have Faces, bk 2, ch. 4

3. THE INCONSOLABLE LONGING

If I find in myself a desire which no experience in this world can satisfy, the most probable explanation is that I was made for another world.

Mere Christianity, bk 3, ch. 10

How could an idiotic universe have produced creatures whose mere dreams are so much stronger, better, subtler than itself? . . . Do fish complain of the sea for being wet? Or if they did, would that fact itself not strongly suggest that they had not always been, or would not always be, purely aquatic creatures? If you are really a product of a materialistic universe, how is it that you don't feel at home there?

Encounter with Light

It now seemed that . . . the deepest thirst within him was not adapted to the deepest nature of the world.

The Pilgrim's Regress, bk 8, ch. 6

In speaking of this desire for our own far-off country, which we find in ourselves even now, I feel a certain shyness. I am almost committing an indecency. I am trying to rip open the inconsolable secret in each one of you—the secret which hurts so much that you take your revenge on it by calling it names like Nostalgia and Romanticism and Adolescence. . . . Our commonest expedient is to call it beauty and behave as if that had settled the matter. Wordsworth's expedient was to identify it with certain moments in his own past. But all this is a cheat. If Wordsworth had gone back to those moments in the past, he would not have found the thing itself, but only the reminder of it; what he remembered would turn out to be itself a remembering. The books or the music in which we thought the beauty was located will betray us if we trust to them; it was not *in* them, it only came *through* them, and what came through them was longing. These things—the beauty, the memory of our own past—are good images of what we really desire; but if they are mistaken for the thing itself they turn into dumb idols, breaking the hearts of their worshippers. For they are not the thing itself; they are only the scent of a flower we have not found, the echo of a tune we have not heard, news from a country we have never yet visited. . . . The sense that in this universe we are treated as strangers, the longing to be acknowledged, to meet with some response, to bridge some chasm that yawns between us and reality, is part of our inconsolable secret. . . .

Our lifelong nostalgia, our longing to be reunited with something in the universe from which we now feel cut off, to be on the inside of some door which we have always seen from the outside, is no mere neurotic fancy, but the truest index of our real situation.

Transposition and Other Addresses, ch. 2.

'Chewing the cud of lusts which are despair
And fill not, . . .'

Dymer, canto 9, st. 8

I perceived (and this was a wonder of wonders) that just as I had been wrong in supposing that I really desired the Garden of the Hesperides, so also I had been equally wrong in supposing that I desired Joy itself. Joy itself, considered simply as an event in my own mind, turned out to be of no value at all. All the value lay in that of which Joy was the desiring. And that object, quite clearly, was no state of my own mind or body at all. In a way, I had proved this by elimination. I had tried everything in my own mind and body; as it were, asking myself, 'Is it this you want? Is it this?' Last of all I had asked if Joy itself was what I wanted; and, labelling it 'aesthetic experience', had pretended I could answer Yes. But that answer too had broken down. Inexorably Joy proclaimed, 'You want—

I myself am your want of—something other, outside, not you
nor any state of you.' I did not yet ask, Who is the desired?
only What is it? But this brought me already into the region of
awe, for I thus understood that in deepest solitude there is a road
right out of the self, a commerce with something which, by
refusing to identify itself with any object of the senses, or anything whereof we have biological or social need, or anything
imagined, or any state of our own minds, proclaims itself sheerly
objective. Far more objective than bodies, for it is not, like
them, clothed in our senses; the naked Other, imageless (though
our imagination salutes it with a hundred images), unknown,
undefined, desired.

Surprised by Joy, ch. 14

Do what they will, then, we remain conscious of a desire
which no natural happiness will satisfy. But is there any reason
to suppose that reality offers any satisfaction to it? . . . A man's
physical hunger does not prove that that man will get any
bread; he may die of starvation on a raft in the Atlantic. But
surely a man's hunger does prove that he comes of a race which
repairs its body by eating and inhabits a world where eatable
substances exist. In the same way, though I do not believe (I
wish I did) that my desire for Paradise proves that I shall enjoy
it, I think it a pretty good indication that such a thing exists and
that some men will. A man may love a woman and not win
her; but it would be very odd if the phenomenon called 'falling
in love' occurred in a sexless world.

Transposition and Other Addresses, ch. 2

We are born helpless. As soon as we are fully conscious we
discover loneliness. . . .
Our whole being by its very nature is one vast need; incomplete, preparatory, empty yet cluttered, crying out for
Him who can untie things that are now knotted together and
tie up things that are still dangling loose.

The Four Loves, ch. 1

A music that resembled
Some earlier music
That men are born remembering.

'Vowels and Sirens', *Poems*

'It was when I was happiest that I longed most. . . . The sweetest thing in all my life has been the longing . . . to find the place where all the beauty came from.'

Till We Have Faces, bk 1, ch. 7

She wanted comfort but she wanted it, if possible, without going out to St. Anne's, without meeting this Fisher-King man and getting drawn into his orbit.

That Hideous Strength, ch. 6

There is a kind of happiness and wonder that makes you serious. It is too good to waste on jokes.

The Last Battle, ch. 15

The very nature of Joy makes nonsense of our common distinction between having and wanting. There, to have is to want and to want is to have. Thus, the very moment when I longed to be so stabbed again, was itself again such a stabbing.

Surprised by Joy, ch. 11

From that first moment in the schoolroom at Chartres my secret, imaginative life began to be so important and so distinct from my outer life that I almost have to tell two separate stories. The two lives do not seem to influence each other at all. Where there are hungry wastes, starving for Joy, in the one, the other may be full of cheerful bustle and success; or again, where the outer life is miserable, the other may be brimming over with ecstasy.

Ibid., ch. 5

About death I go through different moods, but the times when I can *desire* it are never, I think, those when this world seems harshest. On the contrary, it is just when there seems to be most of Heaven already here that I come nearest to longing for a *patria*. It is the bright frontispiece which whets one to read the story itself. All joy (as distinct from mere pleasure, still more amusement) emphasises our pilgrim status; always reminds, beckons, awakens desire. Our best havings are wantings.

Letters (5 November 1959)

There have been times when I think we do not desire heaven; but more often I find myself wondering whether, in our heart of hearts, we have ever desired anything else . . . It is the secret signature of each soul, the incommunicable and unappeasable want, the thing we desired before we met our wives or made our friends or chose our work, and which we shall still desire on our deathbeds, when the mind no longer knows wife or friend or work. . . .

All your life an unattainable ecstasy has hovered just beyond the grasp of your consciousness. The day is coming when you will wake to find, beyond all hope, that you have attained it, or else, that it was within your reach and you have lost it forever.

The Problem of Pain, ch. 10

I shall arise and leave both friends and home
And over many lands a pilgrim go
    Through alien woods and foam,

Seeking the last steep edges of the earth
Whence I may leap into that gulf of light
Wherein, before my narrowing Self had birth,
    Part of me lived aright.

'Our Daily Bread', *Spirits in Bondage*

Dance and game *are* frivolous, unimportant down here; for 'down here' is not their natural place. Here, they are a moment's rest from the life we were placed here to live. But in this world everything is upside down. That which, if it could be prolonged here, would be a truancy, is likest that which in a better country is the End of ends. Joy is the serious business of Heaven.

Letters to Malcolm, ch. 17

'It does not always take the form of an Island. The Landlord sends pictures of many different kinds. What is universal is not the particular picture, but the arrival of some message, not perfectly intelligible, which wakes this desire and sets men longing for something East or West of the world; something possessed, if at all, only in the act of desiring it, and lost so quickly that the craving itself becomes craved; something that tends inevitably to be confused with common or even with vile satisfactions lying close to hand, yet which is able, if any man faithfully live through the dialectic of its successive births and deaths, to lead him at last where true joys are to be found.'

The Pilgrim's Regress, bk 8, ch. 9

'You would not have called to me unless I had been calling to you,' said the Lion.

The Silver Chair, ch. 2

I know now, Lord, why you utter no answer. You are yourself the answer. Before your face questions die away. What other answer would suffice? Only words, words; to be led out to battle against other words.

Till We Have Faces, bk 2, ch. 4

In reading Chesterton, as in reading MacDonald, I did not know what I was letting myself in for. A young man who wishes to remain a sound Atheist cannot be too careful of his reading. There are traps everywhere—'Bibles laid open,

millions of surprises,' as Herbert says, 'fine nets and stratagems.'
God is, if I may say it, very unscrupulous.

Surprised by Joy, ch. 12

4. THE FREE SELF

Thus, and not otherwise, the world was made. Either something or nothing must depend on individual choices.

Perelandra, ch. 11

The sin, both of men and of angels, was rendered possible by the fact that God gave them free will: thus surrendering a portion of His omnipotence (it is again a deathlike or descending movement) because He saw that from a world of free creatures, even though they fell, He could work out (and this is the re-ascent) a deeper happiness and a fuller splendour than any world of automata would admit.

Miracles, ch. 14

The freedom of a creature must mean freedom to choose: and choice implies the existence of things to choose between. A creature with no environment would have no choices to make: so that freedom, like self-consciousness (if they are not, indeed, the same thing) again demands the presence to the self of something other than the self.

The Problem of Pain, ch. 2

If a man travelling in one direction is having a journey down hill, a man going in the opposite direction must be going up hill. If even a pebble lies where I want it to lie, it cannot, except by a coincidence, be where you want it to lie. . . .

We can, perhaps, conceive of a world in which God corrected the results of this abuse of free-will by His creatures at every moment: so that a wooden beam became soft as grass when it was used as a weapon, and the air refused to obey me if I attempted to set up in it the sound waves that carry lies or insults. But such a world would be one in which wrong actions were impossible, and in which, therefore, freedom of the will would be void.

Ibid.

In a game of chess you can make certain arbitrary concessions to your opponent, which stand to the ordinary rules of the game as miracles stand to the laws of nature. You can deprive yourself of a castle, or allow the other man sometimes to take back a move made inadvertently. But if you conceded everything that at any moment happened to suit him—if all his moves were revocable and if all your pieces disappeared whenever their position on the board was not to his liking— then you could not have a game at all. So it is with the life of souls in a world: fixed laws, consequences unfolding by causal necessity, the whole natural order, are at once the limits within which their common life is confined and also the sole condition under which any such life is possible. Try to exclude the possibility of suffering which the order of nature and the existence of free-wills involve, and you find that you have excluded life itself.

Ibid.

Some people think they can imagine a creature which was free but had no possibility of going wrong; I cannot. If a thing is free to be good it is also free to be bad. And free will is what has made evil possible. Why, then, did God give them free will? Because free will, though it makes evil possible, is also the only thing that makes possible any love or goodness or joy worth having. A world of automata—of creatures that worked like machines—would hardly be worth creating. The happiness which God designs for His higher creatures is the happiness of being freely, voluntarily united to Him and to each other in an ecstasy of love and delight compared with which the most rapturous love between a man and a woman on this earth is mere milk and water. And for that they must be free.

If God thinks this state of war in the universe a price worth paying for free will—that is, for making a live world in which creatures can do real good or harm and something of real importance can happen, instead of a toy world which only moves when He pulls the strings—then we may take it it is worth paying.

Mere Christianity, bk 2, ch. 3

When we have understood about free will, we shall see how silly it is to ask, as somebody once asked me: 'Why did God make a creature of such rotten stuff that it went wrong?' The better stuff a creature is made of—the cleverer and stronger and freer it is—then the better it will be if it goes right, but also the worse it will be if it goes wrong. A cow cannot be very good or very bad; a dog can be both better and worse; a child better and worse still; an ordinary man, still more so; a man of genius, still more so; a superhuman spirit best—or worst—of all.

Ibid.

I would say that the most deeply compelled action is also the freest action. By that I mean, no part of you is outside the action. It is a paradox.

'I Was Decided Upon', *Decision* (September 1963)

A person cannot help thinking and speaking of himself as ... two people, one of whom can act upon and observe the other. ... And of course this shadowy inner accomplice has all the same properties as an external one; he too is a witness against you, a potential blackmailer, one who inflicts shame and fear.

Studies in Words, ch. 8, sec. 4

Until you have given up your self to Him you will not have a real self. . . .

Nothing that you have not given away will ever be really yours. Nothing in you that has not died will ever be raised from the dead. Look for yourself, and you will find in the long run only hatred, loneliness, despair, rage, ruin, and decay. But look for Christ and you will find Him, and with Him everything else thrown in.

Mere Christianity, bk 4, ch. 11

The mould under the bushes, the moss on the path, and the little brick border, were not visibly changed. But they were changed. A boundary had been crossed. She had come into a world, or into a Person, or into the presence of a Person. Something expectant, patient, inexorable, met her with no veil or protection between. . . . This demand which now pressed upon her was not, even by analogy, like any other demand. It was the origin of all right demands and contained them. In its light you could understand them; but from them you could know nothing of it. There was nothing, and never had been anything, like this. And now there was nothing except this. Yet also, everything had been like this; only by being like this had anything existed. In this height and depth and breadth the little idea of herself which she had hitherto called *me* dropped down and vanished, unfluttering, into bottomless distance, like a bird in a space without air. . . .

The largest thing that had ever happened to her had, apparently, found room for itself in a moment of time too short to be called time at all.

That Hideous Strength, ch. 14

5. THE CHILD AND CHILDLIKENESS

Critics who treat *adult* as a term of approval, instead of as a

merely descriptive term, cannot be adult themselves. To be
concerned about being grown up, to admire the grown up
because it is grown up, to blush at the suspicion of being childish; these things are the marks of childhood and adolescence.
... When I was ten, I read fairy tales in secret and would have
been ashamed if I had been found doing so. Now that I am
fifty I read them openly. When I became a man I put away
childish things, including the fear of childishness and the desire
to be very grown up.

> 'On Three Ways of Writing for Children',
> *Of Other Worlds*

Only those adults who have retained, with whatever addi-
tions and enrichments, their first childish response to poetry
unimpaired, can be said to have grown up at all. Mere change
is not growth. Growth is the synthesis of change and continuity, and where there is no continuity there is no growth. To
hear some critics, one would suppose that a man had to lose
his nursery appreciation of *Gulliver* before he acquired his
mature appreciation of it. It is not so. If it were, the whole
concept of maturity, of ripening, would be out of place.

> *They Asked for a Paper*, ch. 2

The moral you put in is likely to be a platitude, or even a
falsehood, skimmed from the surface of your consciousness. It
is impertinent to offer the children that. ... The only moral
that is of any value is that which arises inevitably from the
whole cast of the author's mind. ... The child as reader is
neither to be patronized nor idolized: we talk to him as man
to man. But the worst attitude of all would be the professional
attitude which regards children in the lump as a sort of raw
material which we have to handle.

> 'On Three Ways of Writing for Children',
> *Of Other Worlds*

The boy does not despise real woods because he has read of enchanted woods: the reading makes all real woods a little enchanted . . . the boy reading the fairy tale desires and is happy in the very fact of desiring. For his mind has not been concentrated on himself, as it often is in the more realistic story.

Ibid.

II

THE MORAL WORLD

1. THE 'TAO'

These are the two points I wanted to make. First, that human beings, all over the earth, have this curious idea that they ought to behave in a certain way, and cannot really get rid of it. Secondly, that they do not in fact behave in that way. They know the Law of Nature; they break it. These two facts are the foundation of all clear thinking about ourselves and the universe we live in.

Mere Christianity, bk 1, ch. 1

Truth and falsehood are opposed; but truth is the norm not of truth only but of falsehood also.

The Allegory of Love, ch. 7, sec. 2

The Chinese also speak of a great thing (the greatest thing) called the *Tao*. It is the reality beyond all predicates, the abyss that was before the Creator Himself. It is Nature, it is the Way, the Road. It is the Way in which the universe goes on, the Way in which things everlastingly emerge, stilly and tranquilly, into space and time. It is also the Way which every man should tread in imitation of that cosmic and supercosmic progression, conforming all activities to that great exemplar.

. . . Those who know the *Tao* can hold that to call children delightful or old men venerable is not simply to record a psychological fact about our own parental or filial emotions at the moment, but to recognize a quality which *demands* a certain response from us whether we make it or not.

The Abolition of Man, ch. 1

If nothing is self-evident, nothing can be proved. Similarly if nothing is obligatory for its own sake, nothing is obligatory at all.

Ibid., ch. 2

This thing which I have called for convenience the *Tao*, and which others may call Natural Law or Traditional Morality or the First Principles of Practical Reason or the First Platitudes, is not one among a series of possible systems of value. It is the sole source of all value judgements. If it is rejected, all value is rejected. If any value is retained, it is retained. The effort to refute it and raise a new system of value in its place is self-contradictory. There never has been, and never will be, a radically new judgement of value in the history of the world. What purport to be new systems or (as they now call them) 'ideologies', all consist of fragments from the *Tao* itself, arbitrarily wrenched from their context in the whole and then swollen to madness in their isolation, yet still owing to the *Tao* and to it alone such validity as they possess. If my duty to my parents is a superstition, then so is my duty to posterity. If justice is a superstition, then so is my duty to my country or my race. If the pursuit of scientific knowledge is a real value, then so is conjugal fidelity. The rebellion of new ideologies against the *Tao* is a rebellion of the branches against the tree: if the rebels could succeed they would find that they had destroyed themselves. The human mind has no more power of inventing a new value than of imagining a new primary colour, or, indeed, of creating a new sun and a new sky for it to move in. . . .

Outside the *Tao* there is no ground for criticizing either the *Tao* or anything else.

Ibid.

One could indeed say of [the *Tao*] *genitum, non factum*, for is not the *Tao* the Word Himself, considered from a particular point of view?

Letter in Clyde S. Kilby's
The Christian World of C. S. Lewis

Until modern times no thinker of the first rank ever doubted that our judgements of value were rational judgements or that what they discovered was objective. It was taken for granted that in temptation passion was opposed, not to some sentiment, but to reason. Thus Plato thought, thus Aristotle, thus Hooker, Butler and Doctor Johnson. The modern view is very different. It does not believe that value judgements are really judgements at all. They are sentiments, or complexes, or attitudes, produced in a community by the pressure of its environment and its traditions, and differing from one community to another. To say that a thing is good is merely to express our feeling about it; and our feeling about it is the feeling we have been socially conditioned to have. . . . Unless the measuring rod is independent of the things measured, we can do no measuring. . . . The human mind has no more power of inventing a new value than of planting a new sun in the sky or a new primary colour in the spectrum. . . .

'The Poison of Subjectivism',
Christian Reflections

Does a permanent moral standard preclude progress? On the contrary, except on the supposition of a changeless standard, progress is impossible. If good is a fixed point, it is at least possible that we should get nearer and nearer to it, but if the terminus is as mobile as the train, how can the train progress towards it? Our ideas of the good may change, but they cannot change either for the better or the worse if there is no absolute and immutable good to which they can approximate or from which they can recede. We can go on getting a sum more and more nearly right only if the one perfectly right answer is 'stagnant'. . . .

If 'good' means only the local ideology, how can those who invent the local ideology be guided by any idea of good themselves? The very idea of freedom presupposes some objective moral law which overarches rulers and ruled alike. . . .

Unless we return to the crude and nursery-like belief in objective values, we perish.

Ibid.

You can be good for the mere sake of goodness; you cannot be bad for the mere sake of badness. You can do a kind action when you are not feeling kind and when it gives you no pleasure, simply because kindness is right; but no one ever did a cruel action simply because cruelty is wrong—only because cruelty was pleasant or useful to him. In other words badness cannot succeed even in being bad in the same way in which goodness is good. Goodness is, so to speak, itself: badness is only spoiled goodness. And there must be something good first before it can be spoiled. We called sadism a sexual perversion; but you must first have the idea of a normal sexuality before you can talk of its being perverted; and you can see which is the perversion, because you can explain the perverted from the normal, and cannot explain the normal from the perverted. . . . In order to be bad he must have good things to want and then to pursue in the wrong way: he must have impulses which were originally good in order to be able to pervert them.

Mere Christianity, bk 2, ch. 2

The classic expositions of the doctrine that the world's miseries are compatible with its creation and guidance by a wholly good Being come from Boethius waiting in prison to be beaten to death and from St. Augustine meditating on the sack of Rome. . . .

If evil has the same kind of reality as good, the same auto-nomy and completeness, our allegiance to good becomes the arbitrarily chosen loyalty of a partisan. A sound theory of value demands something very different. It demands that good should be original and evil a mere perversion; that good should be the tree and evil the ivy; that good should be able to see all round evil (as when sane men understand lunacy) while evil cannot retaliate in kind; that good should be able to exist on its own while evil requires the good on which it is parasitic in order to continue its parasitic existence.

The consequences of neglecting this are serious. It means believing that bad men like badness as such, in the same way in which good men like goodness. . . .

Badness is not even bad *in the same way* in which goodness is good. . . . The first hazy idea of *devil* must, if we begin to think, be analysed into the more precise ideas of 'fallen' and 'rebel' angel. . . . if Michael is really in the right and Satan really in the wrong this must mean that they stand in two different relations to somebody or something far further back, to the ultimate ground of reality itself.

'Evil and God', *The Spectator* (7 February 1941)

My argument against God was that the universe seemed so cruel and unjust. But how had I got this idea of *just* and *unjust*? A man does not call a line crooked unless he has some idea of a straight line. What was I comparing this universe with when I called it unjust? If the whole show was bad and senseless from A to Z, so to speak, why did I, who was supposed to be part of the show, find myself in such violent reaction against it? A man feels wet when he falls into water, because man is not a water animal: a fish would not feel wet. Of course I could have given up my idea of justice by saying it was nothing but a private idea of my own. But if I did that, then my argument against God collapsed too—for the argument depended on say-ing that the world was really unjust, not simply that it did not happen to please my private fancies. Thus in the very act of trying to prove that God did not exist—in other words, that the whole of reality was senseless—I found I was forced to assume that one part of reality—namely my idea of justice— was full of sense. Consequently atheism turns out to be too simple. If the whole universe has no meaning, we should never have found out that it has no meaning: just as, if there were no light in the universe and therefore no creatures with eyes, we should never know it was dark. *Dark* would be without meaning.

Mere Christianity, bk 2, ch. 1

There is nothing irrational in exercising other powers than our reason. . . . It is rational not to reason, or not to limit one-self to reason, in the wrong place; and the more rational a man is the better he knows this. . . .

We should expect to find in the Church an element which unbelievers will call irrational and which believers will call supra-rational. There ought to be something in it opaque to our reason though not contrary to it. . . . The Church of England can remain a church only if she retains this opaque element. If we abandon that, if we retain only what can be justified by standards of prudence and convenience at the bar of enlightened common sense, then we exchange revelation for that old wraith Natural Religion.

'Notes on the Way',
Time and Tide (14 August 1948)

'If anyone argues with them they say that he is rationalizing his own desires, and therefore need not be answered. But if anyone listens to them they will then argue themselves to show that their own doctrines are true.'

The Pilgrim's Regress, bk 4, ch. 4

It would be impossible to accept naturalism itself if we really and consistently believed naturalism. For naturalism is a system of thought. But for naturalism all thoughts are mere events with irrational causes. . . .

Perhaps this may be even more simply put in another way. Every particular thought (whether it is a judgment of fact or a judgment of value) is always and by all men discounted the moment they believe that it can be explained, without remainder, as the result of irrational causes. Whenever you know what the other man is saying is wholly due to his complexes or to a bit of bone pressing on his brain, you cease to attach any importance to it. But if naturalism were true then all thoughts whatever would be wholly the result of irrational causes. . . . It cuts its own throat. . . .

By thinking at all we have claimed that our thoughts are more than mere natural events. All other propositions must be fitted in as best they can round that primary claim.

'A Christian Reply to Professor Price',
Phoenix Quarterly (Autumn 1946)

No doubt, if A is good for its own sake, we may discover by reasoning that, since B is the means to A, therefore B would be a good thing to do. But by what sort of deduction, and from what sort of premises, could we reach the proposition 'A is good for its own sake'? This must be accepted from some other source before the reasoning can begin.

The Discarded Image, ch. 7, sec. D

Can we carry through to the end the view that human thought is *merely* human: that it is simply a zoological fact about *homo sapiens* that he thinks in a certain way: that it in no way reflects (though no doubt it results from) non-human or universal reality? The moment we ask this question, we receive a check. We are at this very point asking whether a certain view of human thought is true. And the view in question is just the view that human thought is *not* true, not a reflection of reality. And this view is itself a thought. In other words, we are asking 'Is the thought that no thoughts are true, itself true?' If we answer Yes, we contradict ourselves. For if all thoughts are untrue then this thought is untrue.

There is therefore no question of a total scepticism about human thought. We are always prevented from accepting total scepticism because it can be formulated only by making a tacit exception in favour of the thought we are thinking at the moment—just as the man who warns the newcomer 'Don't trust anyone in this office' always expects you to trust him at that moment.

'De Futilitate', Christian Reflections

At least one kind of thought—logical thought—cannot be subjective and irrelevant to the real universe: for unless thought is valid we have no reason to believe in the real universe. We reach our knowledge of the universe only by inference. The very object to which our thought is supposed to be irrelevant depends on the relevance of our thought. A universe whose only claim to be believed in rests on the validity of inference must not start telling us that inference is invalid. . . . I conclude then that logic is a real insight into the way in which real things have to exist. In other words, the laws of thought are also the laws of things: of things in the remotest space and the remotest time.

Ibid.

When you are arguing against Him you are arguing against the very power that makes you able to argue at all.

Mere Christianity, bk 2, ch. 3

If we are to continue to make moral judgments (and whatever we say we shall in fact continue) then we must believe that the conscience of man is not a product of Nature. It can be valid only if it is an offshoot of some absolute moral wisdom,

a moral wisdom which exists absolutely 'on its own' and
is not a product of non-moral, non-rational Nature.

Miracles, ch. 5

Morality or duty . . . never yet made a man happy in himself or dear to others. It is shocking, but it is undeniable. We
do not wish either to be, or to live among, people who are
clean or honest or kind as a matter of duty: we want to be, and
to associate with, people who like being clean and honest and
kind. The mere suspicion that what seemed an act of spontaneous friendliness or generosity was really done as a duty subtly
poisons it. In philosophical language, the ethical category is
self-destructive; morality is healthy only when it is trying to
abolish itself. In theological language, no man can be saved by
works.

English Literature in the Sixteenth Century,
bk 2, ch. 1

The truth is, we believe in decency so much—we feel the
Rule or Law pressing on us so—that we cannot bear to face the
fact that we are breaking it, and consequently we try to shift
the responsibility. For you notice that it is only for our bad
behaviour that we find all these explanations. It is only our bad
temper that we put down to being tired or worried or hungry;
we put our good temper down to ourselves. . . .

The moment you say that one set of moral ideas can be
better than another, you are, in fact, measuring them both by a
standard, saying that one of them conforms to that standard
more nearly than the other. But the standard that measures two
things is something different from either. You are, in fact, comparing them both with some Real Morality, admitting that
there is such a thing as a real Right, independent of what
people think and that some people's ideas get nearer to that
real Right than others.

Mere Christianity, bk 1, chs. 1, 2

Supposing you hear a cry for help from a man in danger. You will probably feel two desires—one a desire to give help (due to your herd instinct), the other a desire to keep out of danger (due to the instinct for self-preservation). But you will find inside you, in addition to these two impulses, a third thing which tells you that you ought to follow the impulse to help, and suppress the impulse to run away. Now this thing that judges between two instincts, that decides which should be encouraged, cannot itself be either of them. You might as well say that the sheet of music which tells you, at a given moment, to play one note on the piano and not another, is itself one of the notes on the keyboard. The Moral Law tells us the tune we have to play: our instincts are merely the keys. . . .

The Moral Law is not any one instinct or any set of instincts: it is something which makes a kind of tune (the tune we call goodness or right conduct) by directing the instincts.

Ibid., bk 1, ch. 2

One man said to me, 'Three hundred years ago people in England were putting witches to death. Was that what you call the Rule of Human Nature or Right Conduct?' But surely the reason we do not execute witches is that we do not believe there are such things. If we did—if we really thought that there were people going about who had sold themselves to the devil and received supernatural powers from him in return and were using these powers to kill their neighbours or drive them mad or bring bad weather, surely we would all agree that if anyone deserved the death penalty, then these filthy quislings did. There is no difference of moral principle here: the difference is simply about matter of fact. It may be a great advance in knowledge not to believe in witches: there is no moral advance in not executing them when you do not think they are there. You would not call a man humane for ceasing to set mousetraps if he did so because he believed there were no mice in the house.

Ibid.

We might try to make out that when you say a man ought not to act as he does, you only mean the same as when you say that a stone is the wrong shape; namely, that what he is doing happens to be inconvenient to you. But that is simply untrue. A man occupying the corner seat in the train because he got there first, and a man who slipped into it while my back was turned and removed my bag, are both equally inconvenient. But I blame the second man and do not blame the first. I am not angry—except perhaps for a moment before I come to my senses—with a man who trips me up by accident; I am angry with a man who tries to trip me up even if he does not succeed. Yet the first has hurt me and the second has not.

Ibid., bk 1, ch. 3

The Moral Law does not give us any grounds for thinking that God is 'good' in the sense of being indulgent, or soft, or sympathetic. There is nothing indulgent about the Moral Law. It is as hard as nails. It tells you to do the straight thing and it does not seem to care how painful, or dangerous, or difficult it is to do. If God is like the Moral Law, then He is not soft.

Ibid., bk 1, ch. 5

You can shuffle 'I want' and 'I am forced' and 'I shall be well advised' and 'I dare not' as long as you please without getting out of them the slightest hint of 'ought' and 'ought not'. And, once again, attempts to resolve the moral experience into something else always presuppose the very thing they are trying to explain—as when a famous psycho-analyst deduces it from prehistoric parricide. If the parricide produced a sense of guilt, that was because men felt that they ought not to have committed it: if they did not so feel, it could produce no sense of guilt. Morality, like numinous awe, is a jump; in it, man goes beyond anything that can be 'given' in the facts of experience. And it has one characteristic too remarkable to be ignored. The moralities accepted among men may differ—though not, at bottom, so widely as is often claimed—but they all agree in prescribing a behaviour which their adherents fail to practise. All men alike stand condemned, not by alien codes of ethics, but by their own, and all men therefore are conscious of guilt. ... This consciousness is neither a logical, nor an illogical, inference from the facts of experience; if we did not bring it to our experience we could not find it there. It is either inexplicable illusion, or else revelation.

The Problem of Pain, ch. 1

Even among ancient authors the same paradox [of good sense and religious conviction] was to be found. The most religious (Plato, Aeschylus, Virgil) were clearly those on whom I could really feed. On the other hand, those writers who did not suffer from religion and with whom in theory my sympathy ought to have been complete—Shaw and Wells and Mill and Gibbon and Voltaire—all seemed a little thin; what as boys we called 'tinny'. It wasn't that I didn't like them. They were all (especially Gibbon) entertaining; but hardly more. There seemed to be no depth in them. They were too simple. The roughness and density of life did not appear in their books.

Surprised by Joy, ch. 14

God may be more than moral goodness: He is not less. The road to the promised land runs past Sinai. The moral law may exist to be transcended: but there is no transcending it for those who have not first admitted its claims upon them and then tried with all their strength to meet that claim, and fairly and squarely faced the fact of their failure.

The Problem of Pain, ch. 4

It seems that there is a general rule in the moral universe which may be formulated 'The higher, the more in danger'. The 'average sensual man' who is sometimes unfaithful to his wife, sometimes tipsy, always a little selfish, now and then (within the law) a trifle sharp in his deals, is certainly, by ordinary standards, a 'lower' type than the man whose soul is filled with some great Cause, to which he will subordinate his appetites, his fortune, and even his safety. But it is out of the second man that something really fiendish can be made; an Inquisitor, a Member of the Committee of Public Safety. It is great men, potential saints, not little men, who become merciless fanatics. Those who are readiest to die for a cause may easily become those who are readiest to kill for it. . . . We must not over-value the relative harmlessness of the little, sensual, frivolous people. They are not above, but below, some temptations.

Reflections on the Psalms, ch. 3

Of all bad men religious bad men are the worst. Of all created beings the wickedest is one who originally stood in the immediate presence of God.

Ibid.

Of all tyrannies a tyranny sincerely exercised for the good of its victims may be the most oppressive. It may be better to live under robber barons than under omnipotent moral busybodies.

'The Humanitarian Theory of Punishment',
Res Judicatae (June 1953)

A theory of punishment which is purely exemplary or purely reformatory, or both, is shockingly immoral. Only the concept of desert connects punishment with morality at all. If deterrence is all that matters, the execution of an innocent man, provided the public think him guilty, would be fully justified. If reformation alone is in question, then there is nothing against painful and compulsory reform for all our defects, and a Government which believes Christianity to be a neurosis will have a perfectly good right to hand us all over to their straighteners for 'cure' tomorrow.

Letter in *Church Times* (1 December 1961)

When we cease to consider what the criminal deserves and consider only what will cure him or deter others, we have tacitly removed him from the sphere of justice altogether; instead of a person, a subject of rights, we now have a mere object, a patient, a 'case'.

'The Humanitarian Theory of Punishment',
Res Judicatae (June 1953)

'Do you place yourself in the obedience,' said the Director, 'in obedience to Maleldil?'

'Sir,' said Jane, 'I know nothing of Maleldil. But I place myself in obedience to you.'

'It is enough for the present,' said the Director. 'This is the courtesy of Deep Heaven: that when you mean well, He always takes you to have meant better than you knew. It will not be enough for always. He is very jealous. He will have you for no one but Himself in the end. But for tonight, it is enough.'

That Hideous Strength, ch. 10

'Those that hate goodness are sometimes nearer than those that know nothing at all about it and think they have it already.'

The Great Divorce, ch. 9

2. REALITY

'Suppose we *have* only dreamed, or made up, all those things—trees and grass and sun and moon and stars and Aslan himself. Suppose we have. Then all I can say is that, in that case, the made-up things seem a good deal more important than the real ones. Suppose this black pit of a kingdom of yours *is* the only world. Well, it strikes me as a pretty poor one. And that's a funny thing, when you come to think of it. We're just babies making up a game, if you're right. But four babies playing a game can make a play-world which licks your real world hollow. That's why I'm going to stand by the play world. I'm on Aslan's side even if there isn't any Aslan to lead it. I'm going to live as like a Narnian as I can even if there isn't any Narnia.'

The Silver Chair, ch. 12

Don't talk to me of the 'illusions' of memory. Why should what we see at the moment be more 'real' than what we see from ten years' distance? It is indeed an illusion to believe that the blue hills on the horizon would still look blue if you went to them. But the fact they are blue five miles away, and the fact that they are green when you are on them, are equally good facts.

Letters to Malcolm, ch. 22

Certain things, if not seen as lovely or detestable, are not being correctly seen at all.

A Preface to 'Paradise Lost', ch. 8

The mere stream of consciousness is for [some people] the reality and it is the special function of poetry to remove the elaborations of civility and get at 'life' in the raw. Hence (in part) the popularity of such a work as *Ulysses*. In my opinion this whole type of criticism is based on an error. . . . It can very easily be shown that the unselective chaos of images and momentary desires which introspection discovers is not the essential characteristic of consciousness. For consciousness is, from the outset, selective, and ceases when selection ceases. . . . The highly selective consciousness enjoyed by fully alert men, with all its builded sentiments and consecrated ideals, has as much claim to be called real as the drowsy chaos, and more. That this chaos may furnish hints for a psychologist's diagnosis, I do not deny. But to conclude thence that in it we reach the reality of the mind is like thinking that the readings of a clinical thermometer or the flayed arms in a medical text book give us a specially 'real' view of the body. . . . There may be a place for literature which tries to exhibit what we are doing when will and reason and attention and organized imagination are all off duty and sleep has not yet supervened. But I believe that if we regard such literature as specially realistic we are falling into illusion.

Ibid., ch. 19

At every stage of religious development man may rebel, if not without violence to his own nature, yet without absurdity. He can close his spiritual eyes against the Numinous, if he is prepared to part company with half the great poets and prophets of his race, with his own childhood, with the richness and depth of uninhibited experience. He can regard the moral law as an illusion, and so cut himself off from the common ground of humanity. He can refuse to identify the Numinous with the righteous, and remain a barbarian, worshipping sexuality, or the dead, or the life-force, or the future. But the cost is heavy. And when we come to the last step of all, the historical Incarnation, the assurance is strongest of all. The story is strangely like many myths which have haunted religion from the first, and yet it is not like them. It is not transparent to the reason: we could not have invented it ourselves. It has not the suspicious *a priori* lucidity of Pantheism or of Newtonian physics. . . . If any message from the core of reality ever were to reach us, we should expect to find in it just that unexpectedness, that wilful, dramatic anfractuosity which we find in the Christian faith. It has the master touch—the rough, male taste of reality, not made by us, or, indeed, for us, but hitting us in the face.

The Problem of Pain, ch. 1

Reality, in fact, is usually something you could not have guessed. That is one of the reasons I believe Christianity. It is a religion you could not have guessed. If it offered us just the kind of universe we had always expected, I should feel we were making it up. But, in fact, it is not the sort of thing anyone would have made up. It has just that queer twist about it that real things have.

Mere Christianity, bk 2, ch. 2

Human intellect is incurably abstract. Pure mathematics is the type of successful thought. Yet the only realities we experience are concrete—this pain, this pleasure, this dog, this man. While we are loving the man, bearing the pain, enjoying the pleasure, we are not intellectually apprehending Pleasure, Pain or Personality. When we begin to do so, on the other hand, the concrete realities sink to the level of mere instances or examples; we are no longer dealing with them, but with that which they exemplify. This is our dilemma—either to taste and not to know or to know and not to taste—or, more strictly, to lack one kind of knowledge because we are in an experience or to lack another kind because we are outside it. As thinkers we are cut off from what we think about; as tasting, touching, willing, loving, hating, we do not clearly understand. The more lucidly we think, the more we are cut off: the more deeply we enter into reality, the less we can think. You cannot *study* Pleasure in the moment of the nuptial embrace, nor repentance while repenting, nor analyse the nature of humour while roaring with laughter. But when else can you really know these things? 'If only my toothache would stop, I could write another chapter about Pain.' But once it stops, what do I know about pain?

'Myth Became Fact',
World Dominion (Sept.–Oct. 1944)

The enjoyment and the contemplation of our inner activities are incompatible. You cannot hope and also think about hoping at the same moment; for in hope we look to hope's object and we interrupt this by (so to speak) turning round to look at the hope itself. Of course the two activities can and do alternate with great rapidity; but they are distinct and incompatible. . . . The surest means of disarming an anger or a lust (I concluded) was to turn your attention from the girl or the insult and start examining the passion itself. The surest way of spoiling a pleasure was to start examining your satisfaction. But if so, it followed that all introspection is in one respect misleading. In introspection we try to look 'inside ourselves' and see what is going on. But nearly everything that was going on a moment before is stopped by the very act of our turning to look at it. Unfortunately this does not mean that introspection finds nothing. On the contrary, it finds precisely what is left behind by the suspension of all our normal activities; and what is left behind is mainly mental images and physical sensations. The great error is to mistake this mere sediment or track or by-product for the activities themselves. That is how men may come to believe that thought is only unspoken words, or the appreciation of poetry only a collection of mental pictures, when these in reality are what the thought or the appreciation, when interrupted, leave behind.

Surprised by Joy, ch. 14

We are inveterate poets. When a quantity is very great we cease to regard it as a mere quantity. Our imaginations awake. Instead of mere quantity, we now have a quality—the Sublime. But for this, the merely arithmetical greatness of the Galaxy would be no more impressive than the figures in an account book.

Miracles, ch. 7

Have we, apart from our Christian faith, any assurance that the historical events which we regard as momentous coincide with those which would be found momentous if God showed us the whole text and deigned to comment?

'Historicism', *Christian Reflections*

History is a story written by the finger of God.

Ibid.

'This moment contains all moments.'

The Great Divorce, ch. 11

Where, except in the present, can the Eternal be met?

'Historicism', *Christian Reflections*

So many things—nay every real *thing*—is good if only it will be humble and ordinate.

Letters (16 April 1940)

3. HIERARCHY

There are no variations except for those who know a norm, and no subtleties for those who have not grasped the obvious.

An Experiment in Criticism, ch. 10

An accusation always implies a standard. . . . You call a man cruel or idle because you have in mind a standard of kindness or diligence. And while you are making the accusation you have to accept the standard as a valid one. If you begin to doubt the standard you automatically doubt the cogency of your accusation. . . . If nothing is certainly right, then of course it follows that nothing is certainly wrong. . . . If a Brute and Blackguard made the world, then he also made our minds. If he made our minds, he also made that very standard in them whereby we judge him to be a Brute and Blackguard. And how can we trust a standard which comes from such a brutal and blackguardly source? If we reject him, we ought to reject all his works. But one of his works is this very moral standard by which we reject him. If we accept this standard then we are really implying that he is not a Brute and Blackguard. If we reject it, then we have thrown away the only instrument by which we can condemn him.

'De Futilitate', *Christian Reflections*

Every sane and civilised man must have some set of principles by which he chooses to reject some of his desires and to permit others. One man does this on Christian principles, another on hygienic principles, another on sociological principles. The real conflict is not between Christianity and 'nature', but between Christian principle and other principles in the control of 'nature'. For 'nature' (in the sense of natural desire) will have to be controlled anyway, unless you are going to ruin your whole life. The Christian principles are, admittedly, stricter than the others; but then we think you will get help towards obeying them which you will not get towards obeying the others.

Mere Christianity, bk 3, ch. 5

I believe in political equality. But there are two opposite reasons for being a democrat. You may think all men so good that they deserve a share in the government of the commonwealth, and so wise that the commonwealth needs their advice. That is, in my opinion, the false, romantic doctrine of democracy. On the other hand, you may believe fallen men to be so wicked that not one of them can be trusted with any irresponsible power over his fellows.

That I believe to be the true ground of democracy. I do not believe that God created an egalitarian world. I believe the authority of parent over child, husband over wife, learned over simple, to have been as much a part of the original plan as the authority of man over beast. . . .

Equality is for me in the same position as clothes. It is a result of the Fall and the remedy for it. Any attempt to retrace the steps by which we have arrived at egalitarianism and to re-introduce the old authorities on the political level is for me as foolish as it would be to take off our clothes. The Nazi and the Nudist make the same mistake. But it is the naked body, still there beneath the clothes of each one of us, which really lives. It is the hierarchical world, still alive and (very properly) hidden behind a façade of equal citizenship, which is our real concern.

Transposition and Other Addresses, ch. 3

It is idle to say that men are of equal value. If value is taken in a wordly sense—if we mean that all men are equally useful or beautiful or good or entertaining—then it is nonsense. If it means that all are of equal value as immortal souls then I think it conceals a dangerous error. The infinite value of each human soul is not a Christian doctrine. God did not die for man because of some value He perceived in him. The value of each human soul considered simply in itself, out of relation to God, is zero. As St. Paul writes, to have died for valuable men would have been not divine but merely heroic; but God died for sinners. He loved us not because we were lovable, but because He is Love. It may be that He loves all equally—He certainly loved all to the death—and I am not certain what the expression means. If there is equality it is in His love, not in us.

Ibid.

Equality is a quantitative term and therefore love often knows nothing of it. Authority exercised with humility and obedience accepted with delight are the very lines along which our spirits live. Even in the life of the affections, much more in the Body of Christ, we step outside that world which says 'I am as good as you'. It is like turning from a march to a dance. It is like taking off our clothes. We become, as Chesterton said, taller when we bow; we become lowlier when we instruct. It delights me that there should be moments in the services of my own Church when the priest stands and I kneel. As democracy becomes more complete in the outer world and opportunities for reverence are successively removed, the refreshment, the cleansing, and invigorating returns to inequality, which the Church offers us, become more and more necessary.

Ibid.

I reject at once an idea which lingers in the mind of some modern people that cultural activities are in their own right spiritual and meritorious—as though scholars and poets were intrinsically more pleasing to God than scavengers and boot-blacks. I think it was Matthew Arnold who first used the English word *spiritual* in the sense of the German *geistlich*, and so inaugurated this most dangerous and most anti-Christian error. Let us clear it forever from our minds. The work of a Beethoven, and the work of a charwoman, become spiritual on precisely the same condition, that of being offered to God, of being done humbly 'as to the Lord'. This does not, of course, mean that it is for anyone a mere toss-up whether he should sweep rooms or compose symphonies. A mole must dig to the glory of God and a cock must crow.

Ibid., ch. 4

The demand for equality has two sources; one of them is among the noblest, the other is the basest, of human emotions. The noble source is the desire for fair play. But the other source is the hatred of superiority. . . .

Equality (outside mathematics) is a purely social conception. It applies to man as a political and economic animal. It has no place in the world of the mind. Beauty is not democratic; she reveals herself more to the few than to the many. . . . Virtue is not democratic; she is achieved by those who pursue her more hotly than most men. Truth is not democratic; she demands special talents and special industry in those to whom she gives her favours. Political democracy is doomed if it tries to extend its demand for equality into these higher spheres. Ethical, intellectual, or aesthetic democracy is death.

A truly democratic education—one which will preserve democracy—must be, in its own field, ruthlessly aristocratic, shamelessly 'high-brow'. . . .

Democracy demands that little men should not take big ones

too seriously; it dies when it is full of little men who think they are big themselves.

'Notes on the Way',
Time and Tide (29 April 1944)

No man who says *I'm as good as you* believes it. He would not say it if he did. The St Bernard never says it to the toy dog, nor the scholar to the dunce, nor the employable to the bum, nor the pretty woman to the plain. The claim to equality, outside the strictly political field, is made only by those who feel themselves to be in some way inferior. What it expresses is precisely the itching, smarting, writhing awareness of an inferiority which the patient refuses to accept.

And therefore resents. Yes, and therefore resents every kind of superiority in others; denigrates it; wishes its annihilation. Presently he suspects every mere difference of being a claim to superiority. . . . 'Here's a fellow who says he doesn't like hot dogs—thinks himself too good for them, no doubt. . . . If they were honest-to-God all-right Joes they'd be like me. They've no business to be different. It's undemocratic.'

The Screwtape Letters and Screwtape Proposes a Toast, pt II

Cut them all down to a level: all slaves, all ciphers, all nobodies. All equals. Thus Tyrants could practise, in a sense, 'democracy'. But now 'democracy' can do the same work without any tyranny other than her own. No one need now go through the field with a cane. The little stalks will now of themselves bite the tops off the big ones. The big ones are beginning to bite off their own in their desire to Be Like Stalks.

Ibid.

They do not get their qualities from a class: they belong to that class because they have those qualities.

'Delinquents in the Snow',
Time and Tide (7 December 1957)

The modern reader is apt to start from an egalitarian conception; to assume, in fact, that the fair way of dividing a cake between two people is to cut it into two equal pieces. But to this Aristotle, and the most reputable political thinkers between Aristotle's time and Spenser's, would have replied at once 'It all depends who the two people are. If A is twice as good a man as B, then obviously justice means giving A twice as much cake as B. For justice is not equality *simpliciter* but proportional equality.' When this principle is applied to things more important than cakes, justice becomes the art of allotting carefully graded shares of honour, power, liberty and the like to the various ranks of a fixed social hierarchy, and when justice succeeds, she produces a harmony of differences.

The Allegory of Love, ch. 7, sec. 3

. . . . Every duty is a religious duty, and our obligation to perform every duty is therefore absolute. Thus we may have a duty to rescue a drowning man, and perhaps, if we live on a dangerous coast, to learn life-saving so as to be ready for any drowning man when he turns up. It may be our duty to lose our own lives in saving him. But if anyone devoted himself to life-saving in the sense of giving it his total attention—so that he thought and spoke of nothing else and demanded the cessation of all other human activities until everyone had learned to swim—he would be a monomaniac. The rescue of drowning men is, then a duty worth dying for, but not worth living for. . . . He who surrenders himself without reservation to the temporal claims of a nation, or a party, or a class is rendering to Caesar that which, of all things, most emphatically belongs to God: himself. . . .

There is no question of a compromise between the claims of God and the claims of culture, or politics, or anything else. God's claim is infinite and inexorable. You can refuse it: or you can begin to try to grant it. There is no middle way. Yet in spite of this it is clear that Christianity does not exclude any of the ordinary human activities. St. Paul tells people to get on with their jobs. He even assumes that Christians may go to dinner parties, and, what is more, dinner parties given by pagans. . . .

All our merely natural activities will be accepted, if they are offered to God, even the humblest: and all of them, even the noblest, will be sinful if they are not. Christianity does not simply replace our natural life and substitute a new one: it is rather a new organization which exploits, to its own supernatural ends, these natural materials.

Transposition and Other Addresses, ch. 2

4. PROPER USE OF OBJECTS

The first qualification for judging any piece of workmanship from a corkscrew to a cathedral is to know *what* it is—what it was intended to do and how it is meant to be used.

A Preface to 'Paradise Lost', ch. 1

One great piece of mischief has been done by the modern restriction of the word Temperance to the question of drink. It helps people to forget that you can be just as intemperate about lots of other things. A man who makes his golf or his motor-bicycle the centre of his life, or a woman who devotes all her thoughts to clothes or bridge or her dog, is being just as 'intemperate' as someone who gets drunk every evening. Of course, it does not show on the outside so easily: bridge-mania or golf-mania do not make you fall down in the middle of the road. But God is not deceived by externals.

Mere Christianity, bk 3, ch. 2

If we encourage others, or ourselves, to hear, see, or read great art on the ground that it is a *cultured* thing to do, we call into play precisely those elements in us which must be in abeyance before we can enjoy art at all. We are calling up the desire for self-improvement, the desire for distinction, the desire to revolt (from one group) and to agree (with another), and a dozen busy passions which, whether good or bad in themselves, are, in relation to the arts, simply a blinding and paralysing distraction. . . .

Those who read poetry to improve their minds will never improve their minds by reading poetry. For the true enjoyments must be spontaneous and compulsive and look to no remoter end.

The World's Last Night, ch. 3

In religion, as in war and everything else, comfort is the one thing you cannot get by looking for it. If you look for truth, you may find comfort in the end: if you look for comfort you will not get either comfort or truth—only soft soap and wishful thinking to begin with and, in the end, despair.

Mere Christianity, bk 1, ch. 5

The moment good taste knows itself, some of its goodness is lost.

Surprised by Joy, ch. 7

We no more become bad by thinking of badness than we become triangular by thinking about triangles.

A Preface to 'Paradise Lost', ch. 12

Games are essentially for pleasure, but they happen to produce health. They are not likely, however, to produce health if they are played for the sake of it.

Rehabilitations, ch. 4

We have had enough, once and for all, of Hedonism—the gloomy philosophy which says that Pleasure is the only good.

But we have hardly yet begun what may be called *Hedonics*, the science or philosophy of Pleasure.

'Hedonics', *Time and Tide* (16 June 1945)

The woman who makes a dog the centre of her life loses, in the end, not only her human usefulness and dignity but even the proper pleasure of dog-keeping. . . . Every preference of a small good to a great, or a partial good to a total good, involves the loss of the small or partial good for which the sacrifice was made. . . . You can get second things only by putting first things first. . . .

It is impossible, in this context, not to inquire what our own civilization has been putting first for the last thirty years. And the answer is plain. It has been putting itself first. To preserve civilization has been the great aim; the collapse of civilization, the great bugbear. Peace, a high standard of life, hygiene, transport, science and amusement—all these, which are what we usually mean by civilization, have been our ends. . . . How if civilization has been imperilled precisely by the fact that we have made civilization our *summum bonum*. . . . Perhaps civilization will never be safe until we care for something else more than we care for it.

'Notes on the Way',
Time and Tide (27 June 1942)

Many things—such as loving, going to sleep, or behaving unaffectedly—are done worst when we try hardest to do them.

Studies in Medieval and Renaissance Literature,
ch. 9, sec. 2

Conquest is an evil productive of almost every other evil both to those who commit and to those who suffer it.

Ibid., ch. 9, sec. 1

What I like about experience is that it is such an honest thing. You may take any number of wrong turnings; but keep your eyes open and you will not be allowed to go very far before the warning signs appear. You may have deceived yourself, but experience is not trying to deceive you. The universe rings true wherever you fairly test it.

Surprised by Joy, ch. 11

A metaphysic, held by the rulers with the force of a religion, is a bad sign. It forbids them, like the inquisitor, to admit any grain of truth or good in their opponents, it abrogates the ordinary rules of morality, and it gives a seemingly high, super-personal sanction to all the very ordinary human passions by which, like other men, the rulers will frequently be actuated. In a word, it forbids wholesome doubt.

'A Reply to Professor Haldane',
Of Other Worlds

If individuals live only seventy years, then a state, or a nation, or a civilisation, which may last for a thousand years, is more important than an individual. But if Christianity is true, then the individual is not only more important but incomparably more important, for he is everlasting and the life of a state or a civilisation, compared with his, is only a moment.

Mere Christianity, bk 3, ch. 1

Can a mortal ask questions which God finds unanswerable? Quite easily, I should think. All nonsense questions are unanswerable. How many hours are there in a mile? Is yellow square or round? Probably half the questions we ask—half our great theological and metaphysical problems—are like that. . . .

Heaven will solve our problems, but not, I think, by showing us subtle reconciliations between all our apparently contradictory notions. The notions will all be knocked from under our feet. We shall see that there never was any problem.

A Grief Observed, ch. 4

5. RELIGION AND IRRELIGION

I was at this time living, like so many Atheists or Anti-
theists, in a whirl of contradictions. I maintained that God did
not exist. I was also very angry with God for not existing. I was
equally angry with Him for creating a world.

Surprised by Joy, ch. 7

The notion that everyone would *like* Christianity to be true,
and therefore all atheists are brave men who have accepted the
defeat of all their deepest desires, is simply impudent nonsense.

Encounter with Light

Men are reluctant to pass over the notion of an abstract and
negative deity to the living God. I do not wonder. Here lies the
deepest tap-root of Pantheism and of the objection to traditional imagery. It was hated not, at bottom, because it pictured
Him as man but because it pictured Him as king, or even as war-
rior. The Pantheist's God does nothing, demands nothing. He
is there if you wish for Him, like a book on a shelf. He will not
pursue you. There is no danger that at any time heaven and
earth should flee away at His glance.

Miracles, ch. 11

The difficulty in preaching Christ in India is that there is no
difficulty. One is up against true Paganism—the best sort of it
as well as the worst—hospitable to all gods, naturally religious,
ready to take any shape but able to retain none.

Letters (30 April 1959)

The god of whom no dogmas are believed is a mere shadow.
He will not produce that fear of the Lord in which wisdom
begins, and, therefore, will not produce that love in which it is
consummated. . . . There is in this minimal religion nothing

that can convince, convert, or (in the higher sense) console: nothing, therefore, which can restore vitality to our civilization. It is not costly enough. It can never be a controller or even a rival to our natural sloth and greed.

'A Christian Reply to Professor Price',
Phoenix Quarterly (Autumn 1946)

Now that I am a Christian I do have moods in which the whole thing looks very improbable: but when I was an atheist I had moods in which Christianity looked terribly probable.

Mere Christianity, bk 3, ch. 11

He has substituted *religion* for God—as if navigation were substituted for arrival, or battle for victory, or wooing for marriage, or in general the means for the end. But even in this present life, there is danger in the very concept of *religion*. It carries the suggestion that this is one more department of life, an extra department added to the economic, the social, the intellectual, the recreational, and all the rest.

Letters to Malcolm, ch. 6

Men who have gods worship those gods; it is the spectators who describe this as 'religion'. The Maenads thought about Dionysus, not about religion. *Mutatis mutandis* this goes for Christians too. The moment a man seriously accepts a deity his interest in 'religion' is at an end. He's got something else to think about. The ease with which we can now get an audience for a discussion of religion does not prove that more people are becoming religious. What it really proves is the existence of a large 'floating vote'. Every conversion will reduce this potential audience.

'Revival or Decay?'
Punch (9 July 1958)

Fascism and Communism, like all other evils, are potent

because of the good they contain or imitate. . . . And of course their occasion is the failure of those who left humanity starved of that particular good. This does not for me alter the conviction that they are very bad indeed.

Letters (17 January 1940)

III

THE BIBLE

Men can read the life of Our Lord (because it is a human life) as nothing but a human life.... Just in the same way Scripture can be read as merely human literature.... For what is required, on all these levels alike, is not merely knowledge but a certain insight; getting the focus right.... One who contended that a poem was nothing but black marks on white paper would be unanswerable if he addressed an audience who couldn't read. Look at it through microscopes, analyse the printer's ink and the paper, study it (in that way) as long as you like; you will never find something over and above all the products of analysis whereof you can say 'This is the poem'. Those who can read, however, will continue to say the poem exists. ...

Taken by a literalist, He will always prove the most elusive of teachers. Systems cannot keep up with that darting illumination. No net less wide than a man's whole heart, nor less fine of mesh than love, will hold the sacred Fish.

Reflections on the Psalms, ch. 11

The Day of Judgement is an idea very familiar, and very dreadful, to Christians.... If there is any concept which cannot by any conjuring be removed from the teaching of Our Lord, it is that of the great separation; the sheep and the goats, the broad way and the narrow, the wheat and the tares, the winnowing fan, the wise and the foolish virgins, the good fish and the refuse, the door closed on the marriage feast, with some inside and some outside in the dark. .... It is from His own words that the picture of 'Doomsday' has come into Christianity.

'The Psalms', *Christian Reflections*

When you accepted the exodus of Israel from Egypt as a type of the soul's escape from sin, you did not on that account abolish the exodus as a historical event.

The Allegory of Love, ch. 5, sec. 2

Some people when they say that a thing is meant 'metaphorically' conclude from this that it is hardly meant at all. They rightly think that Christ spoke metaphorically when he told us to carry the cross: they wrongly conclude that carrying the cross means nothing more than leading a respectable life and subscribing moderately to charities. They reasonably think that hell fire' is a metaphor—and unwisely conclude that it means nothing more serious than remorse. They say that the story of the Fall in *Genesis* is not literal; and then go on to say that it was really a fall upwards—which is like saying that because 'My heart is broken' contains a metaphor, it therefore means 'I feel very cheerful'. This mode of interpretation I regard, frankly, as nonsense. For me the Christian doctrines which are 'metaphorical'—or which have become metaphorical with the increase of abstract thought—mean something which is just as 'supernatural' or shocking after we have removed the ancient imagery as it was before.

Miracles, ch. 10

Books on psychology or economics or politics are as continuously metaphorical as books of poetry or devotion.

Ibid.

Our age has, indeed, coined the expression 'the Bible as literature'. It is very generally implied that those who have rejected its theological pretentions nevertheless continue to enjoy it as a treasure house of English prose. It may be so. There may be people who, not having been forced upon familiarity with it by believing parents, have yet been drawn to it by its literary charms and remained as constant readers. But I never happen to meet them. Perhaps it is because I live in the provinces. But I cannot help suspecting, if I may make an Irish bull, that those who read the Bible as literature do not read the Bible. . . .

Unless the religious claims of the Bible are again acknowledged, its literary claims will, I think, be given only 'mouth honour' and that decreasingly.

They Asked for a Paper, ch. 2

The same divine humility which decreed that God should become a baby at a peasant-woman's breast, and later an arrested field-preacher in the hands of the Roman police, decreed also that He should be preached in a vulgar, prosaic and unliterary language. If you can stomach the one, you can stomach the other. The Incarnation is in that sense an irreverent doctrine: Christianity, in that sense, an incurably irreverent religion. When we expect that it should have come before the World in all the beauty that we now feel in the Authorised Version we are as wide of the mark as the Jews were in expecting that the Messiah would come as a great earthly King. The real sanctity, the real beauty and sublimity of the New Testament (as of Christ's life) are of a different sort: miles deeper or *further in*.

Introduction to J. B. Phillips's *Letters to Young Churches*

And finally, though it may seem a sour paradox—we must sometimes get away from the Authorised Version, if for no other reason, simply *because* it is so beautiful and so solemn. Beauty exalts, but beauty also lulls. Early associations endear but they also confuse. Through that beautiful solemnity the

transporting or horrifying realities of which the Book tells may
come to us blunted and disarmed and we may only sigh with
tranquil veneration when we ought to be burning with shame
or struck dumb with terror or carried out of ourselves by
ravishing hopes and adorations.

Ibid

Odd, the way the less the Bible is read the more it is translated.

Letters (25 May 1962)

It seems to me appropriate, almost inevitable, that when that
great Imagination which in the beginning, for Its own delight
and for the delight of men and angels and (in their proper
mode) of beasts, had invented and formed the whole world
of Nature, submitted to express Itself in human speech, that
speech should sometimes be poetry. For poetry too is a little
incarnation, giving body to what had been before invisible and
inaudible.

Reflections on the Psalms, ch. 1

A visitor from another world who judged humanity simply
by its poetry would get the impression from profane poetry
that we were creatures who lived habitually on a high, level
plateau of consistent passion; from our sacred poetry, and from
it almost alone, would he get any notion of human experience
as it really is, with all its lee-shores and doldrums and rudderless
hithering and thithering.... It is the profane poetry which
assumes attitudes of greater clarity and consistency than inner
experience will really support; it is the sacred poetry which
gives us life in the raw. For whatever else the religious life may
be, it is the fountain of self-knowledge and disillusion, the
safest form of psychoanalysis.

Book review, *Review of English Studies* (January 1941)

The most valuable thing the Psalms do for me is to express the same delight in God which made David dance. ...

[The Psalmists] express a longing for Him, for His mere presence, which comes only to the best Christians or to Christians in their best moments.

Reflections on the Psalms, ch. 5

The dominant impression I get from reading the Psalms is one of antiquity. I seem to be looking into a deep pit of time, but looking through a lens which brings the figures who inhabit that depth up close to my eye. In that momentary proximity they are almost shockingly alien; creatures of unrestrained emotion, wallowing in self-pity, sobbing, cursing, screaming in exultation, clashing uncouth weapons or dancing to the din of strange musical instruments. Yet, side by side with this, there is also a different image in my mind: Anglican choirs, well laundered surplices, soapy boys' faces, hassocks, an organ, prayer-books, and perhaps the smell of new-mown graveyard grass coming in with the sunlight through an open door. Sometimes the one, sometimes the other, impression grows faint, but neither, perhaps, ever quite disappears.

'The Psalms', *Christian Reflections*

[Psalm 119] is a pattern, a thing done like embroidery, stitch by stitch, through long, quiet hours, for love of the subject and for the delight in leisurely, disciplined craftsmanship. ...

This is not priggery nor even scrupulosity; it is the language of a man ravished by a moral beauty.

Reflections on the Psalms, ch. 6

The Psalmists ... give us little landscape. What they do give us, far more sensuously and delightedly than anything I have seen in Greek, is the very feel of weather—weather seen with a real countryman's eyes, enjoyed almost as a vegetable might be supposed to enjoy it.

Ibid., ch. 8

What an admirable thing it is in the divine economy that the sacred literature of the world should have been entrusted to a people whose poetry, depending largely on parallelism, should remain poetry in any language you translate it into.

Letters (16 July 1940)

The question whether miracles occur can never be answered simply by experience. Every event which might claim to be a miracle is, in the last resort, something presented to our senses, something seen, heard, touched, smelled, or tasted. And our senses are not infallible. If anything extraordinary seems to have happened, we can always say that we have been the victims of an illusion. If we hold a philosophy which excludes the supernatural, this is what we always shall say.

Miracles, ch. 1

The divine art of miracle is not an art of suspending the pattern to which events conform but of feeding new events into that pattern. . . .

A miracle is emphatically not an event without cause or without results. Its cause is the activity of God: its results follow according to Natural law. . . . Its peculiarity is that it is not in that way interlocked backwards, interlocked with the previous history of Nature. . . . To find how it is interlocked with the previous history of Nature you must replace both Nature and the miracle in a larger context. Everything *is* connected with everything else: but not all things are connected by the short and straight roads we expected.

Ibid., ch 8

By definition, miracles must of course interrupt the usual course of Nature, but if they are real they must, in the very act of so doing, assert all the more the unity and self-consistency of total reality at some deeper level. They will not be like unmetrical lumps of prose breaking the unity of a poem; they will be like that crowning metrical audacity which, though it may be paralleled nowhere else in the poem, yet, coming just where it does, and effecting just what it effects, is (to those who understand) the supreme revelation of the unity in the poet's conception. .... If Nature brings forth miracles then doubtless it is as 'natural' for her to do so when impregnated by the masculine force beyond her as it is for a woman to bear children to a man.

Ibid.

Theology says to you in effect, 'Admit God and with Him the risk of a few miracles, and I in return will ratify your faith in uniformity as regards the overwhelming majority of events.' The philosophy which forbids you to make uniformity absolute is also the philosophy which offers you solid grounds for believing it to be general, to be *almost* absolute. The Being who threatens Nature's claim to omnipotence confirms her in her lawful occasions. Give us this ha'porth of tar and we will save the ship. The alternative is really much worse. Try to make Nature absolute and you find that her uniformity is not even probable. By claiming too much, you get nothing. You get the deadlock, as in Hume. Theology offers you a working arrangement, which leaves the scientist free to continue his experiments and the Christian to continue his prayers.

Ibid., ch. 13

What cannot be trusted to recur is not material for science: that is why history is not one of the sciences. You cannot find out what Napoleon did at the battle of Austerlitz by asking him to come and fight it again in a laboratory with the same combatants, the same *terrain*, the same weather, and in the same age. You have to go to the records. We have not, in fact, proved that science excludes miracles: we have only proved that the question of miracles, like the innumerable other questions, excludes laboratory treatment.

'A Christian Reply to Professor Price',
Phoenix Quarterly (Autumn 1946)

All the essentials of Hinduism would, I think, remain unimpaired if you subtracted the miraculous, and the same is almost true of Mohammedanism. But you cannot do that with Christianity. It is precisely the story of a great Miracle. A naturalistic Christianity leaves out all that is specifically Christian.

Miracles, ch. 10

IV

THE TRINITY

1. GOD

Not many years ago when I was an atheist, if anyone had asked me, 'Why do you not believe in God?' my reply would have run something like this: 'Look at the universe we live in. By far the greatest part of it consists of empty space, completely dark and unimaginably cold. The bodies which move in this space are so few and so small in comparison with the space itself that even if every one of them were known to be crowded as full as it could hold with perfectly happy creatures, it would still be difficult to believe that life and happiness were more than a by-product to the power that made the universe. ... History is largely a record of crime, war, disease, and terror, with just sufficient happiness interposed to give them, while it lasts, an agonised apprehension of losing it, and, when it is lost, the poignant misery of remembering. Every now and then they improve their condition a little and what we call a civilisation appears. But all civilisations pass away and, even while they remain, inflict peculiar sufferings of their own probably sufficient to outweigh what alleviations they may have brought to the normal pains of man. ... If you ask me to believe that this is the work of a benevolent and omnipotent spirit, I reply that all the evidence points in the opposite direction. Either there is no spirit behind the universe, or else a spirit indifferent to good and evil, or else an evil spirit.'

There was one question which I never dreamed of raising. I

never noticed that the very strength and facility of the pessimists' case at once poses us a problem. If the universe is so bad, or even half so bad, how on earth did human beings ever come to attribute it to the activity of a wise and good Creator?

The Problem of Pain, ch. 1

Looking for God—or Heaven—by exploring space is like reading or seeing all Shakespeare's plays in the hope that you will find Shakespeare as one of the characters or Stratford as one of the places. Shakespeare is in one sense present at every moment in every play. But he is never present in the same way as Falstaff or Lady Macbeth. Nor is he diffused through the play like a gas.

If there were an idiot who thought plays existed on their own, without an author . . . our belief in Shakespeare would not be much affected by his saying, quite truly, that he had studied all the plays and never found Shakespeare in them. . . .

I am not suggesting at all that the existence of God is as easily established as the existence of Shakespeare. My point is that, if God does exist, He is related to the universe more as an author is related to a play than as one object in the universe is related to another. . . .

To some, God is discoverable everywhere; to others, nowhere. Those who do not find Him on earth are unlikely to find Him in space. (Hang it all, we're in space already; every year we go a huge circular tour in space.) But send a saint up in a spaceship and he'll find God in space as he found God on earth. Much depends on the seeing eye.

'The Seeing Eye', *Christian Reflections*

If we fully understand *what* God is we should see that there is no question *whether* He is. It would always have been impossible that He should not exist. He is the opaque centre of all existences, the thing that simply and entirely *is*, the fountain of facthood. And yet, now that He has created, there is a sense in which we must say that He is a particular Thing and even one Thing among others. To say this is not to lessen the immeasurable difference between Him and them. On the contrary, it is to recognise in Him a positive perfection which Pantheism has obscured; the perfection of being creative. He is so brim-full of existence that He can give existence away, can cause things to be, and to be really other than Himself, can make it untrue to say that He is everything.

Miracles, ch. 11

This human life in God is from our point of view a particular period in the history of our world (from the year A.D. one till the Crucifixion). We therefore imagine it is also a period in the history of God's own existence. But God has no history. He is too completely and utterly real to have one. For, of course, to have a history means losing part of your reality (because it had already slipped away into the past) and not yet having another part (because it is still in the future): in fact having nothing but the tiny little present, which has gone before you can speak about it. God forbid we should think God was like that. Even we may hope not to be always rationed in that way.

Mere Christianity, bk 4, ch. 3

My Adversary waived the point. It sank into utter unimportance. He would not argue about it. He only said, 'I am the Lord'; 'I am that I am'; 'I am'.

People who are naturally religious find difficulty in understanding the horror of such a revelation. Amiable agnostics will talk cheerfully about 'man's search for God'. To me, as I then was, they might as well have talked about the mouse's search for the cat.

Surprised by Joy, ch. 14

As long as a man is thinking of God as an examiner who has

set him a sort of paper to do, or as the opposite party in a sort of bargain—as long as he is thinking of claims and counter-claims between himself and God—he is not yet in the right relation to Him. He is misunderstanding what he is and what God is. And he cannot get into the right relation until he has discovered the fact of our bankruptcy.

Mere Christianity, bk 3, ch. 12

We may ignore, but we can nowhere evade, the presence of God. The world is crowded with Him. He walks everywhere *incognito*.

Letters to Malcolm, ch. 14

Why are many people prepared in advance to maintain that, whatever else God may be, He is not the concrete, living, willing, and acting God of Christian theology? I think the reason is as follows. Let us suppose a mystical limpet, a sage among limpets, who (rapt in vision) catches a glimpse of what Man is like. In reporting it to his disciples, who have some vision themselves (though less than he) he will have to use many negatives. He will have to tell them that Man has no shell, is not attached to a rock, is not surrounded by water. And his disciples, having a little vision of their own to help them, do get some idea of Man. But then there come erudite limpets, limpets who write histories of philosophy and give lectures on comparative religion, and who have never had any vision of their own. What they get out of the prophetic limpet's words is simply and solely the negatives. From these, uncorrected by any positive insight, they build up a picture of Man as a sort of amorphous jelly (he has no shell) existing nowhere in particular (he is not attached to a rock) and never taking nourishment (there is no water to drift it towards him). And having a traditional reverence for Man they conclude that to be a famished jelly in a dimensionless void is the supreme mode of existence, and reject as crude, materialistic superstition any doctrine which would attribute to Man a definite shape, a structure, and organs.

Miracles, ch. 11

Bishop Robinson draws a sharp distinction between asking 'Does God exist as a person?' and asking whether ultimate reality is personal. But surely he who says yes to the second question has said yes to the first? Any entity describable without gross abuse of language as God must be ultimate reality, and if ultimate reality is personal, then God is personal.

'Must Our Image of God Go?' *The Observer*
(24 March 1963)

This talk of 'meeting' is, no doubt, anthropomorphic; as if God and I could be face to face, like two fellow-creatures, when in reality He is above me and within me and below me and all about me. That is why it must be balanced by all manner of metaphysical and theological abstractions. But never, here or anywhere else, let us think that while anthropomorphic images are a concession to our weakness, the abstractions are the literal truth. Both are equally concessions; each singly misleading, and the two together mutually corrective. Unless you sit to it very tightly, continually murmuring 'Not thus, not thus, neither is this Thou', the abstraction is fatal. It will make the life of lives inanimate and the love of loves impersonal. The *naïf* image is mischievous chiefly in so far as it holds unbelievers back from conversion. It does believers, even at its crudest, no harm. What soul ever perished for believing that God the Father really has a beard?

Letters to Malcolm, ch. 4

What do you suppose you have gained by substituting the image of a live wire for that of angered majesty? You have shut us all up in despair; for the angry can forgive, and electricity can't.

Ibid., ch. 18

What we must fight against is Pope's maxim

> the first Almighty Cause
> Acts not by partial, but by general laws.

The odd thing is that Pope thought, and all who agree with
him think, that this philosophical theology is an advance
beyond the religion of the child and the savage (and the New
Testament). It seems to them less *naïf* and anthropomorphic.
The real difference, however, is that the anthropomorphism is
more subtly hidden and of a far more disastrous type. . . .

On Pope's view God has to work in the same way. He has
His grand design for the sum of things. Nothing we can say
will deflect it. It leaves Him little freedom (or none?) for
granting, or even for deliberately refusing, our prayers. The
grand design churns out innumerable blessings and curses for
individuals. God can't help that. They're all by-products. . . .

Generalities are the lenses with which our intellects have to
make do. How should God sully the infinite lucidity of this
vision with such make-shifts? One might as well think He had
to consult books of reference, or that, if He ever considered
me individually, He would begin by saying, 'Gabriel, bring me
Mr. Lewis's file.'

Ibid., ch. 10

We cannot see light, though by light we can see things.
Statements about God are extrapolations from the knowledge
of other things which the divine illumination enables us to
know.

The Four Loves, ch. 6

God is basic Fact or Actuality, the source of all other facthood. At all costs therefore He must not be thought of as a
featureless generality. If he exists at all, He is the most concrete
thing there is, the most individual, 'organised and minutely
articulated'. He is unspeakable not by being indefinite but by

being too definite for the unavoidable vagueness of language. . . . Grammatically the things we say of Him are 'metaphorical': but in a deeper sense it is our physical and psychic energies that are mere 'metaphors' of the real Life which is God.

Miracles, ch. 11

His Omnipotence means power to do all that is intrinsically possible, not to do the intrinsically impossible. You may attribute miracles to Him, but not nonsense. This is no limit to His power. If you choose to say 'God can give a creature free-will and at the same time withhold free-will from it', you have not succeeded in saying *anything* about God: meaningless combinations of words do not suddenly acquire meaning simply because we prefix to them the two other words 'God can'. It remains true that all *things* are possible with God: the intrinsic impossibilities are not things but nonentities. It is no more possible for God than for the weakest of His creatures to carry out both of two mutually exclusive alternatives; not because His power meets an obstacle, but because nonsense remains nonsense even when we talk it about God.

The Problem of Pain, ch. 2

Don't bother about the idea that God 'has known for millions of years exactly what you are about to pray'. That isn't what it's like. God is hearing you *now*, just as simply as a mother hears a child. The difference His timelessness makes is that this *now* (which slips away from you even as you say the word *now*) is for Him infinite.

Letters (1 August 1949)

'All things are by Him and for Him. He utters Himself also for His own delight and sees that He is good. He is His own begotten and what proceeds from him is Himself. Blessed be He!'

'All that is made seems planless to the darkened mind, because there are more plans than it looked for. .... Set your eyes on one movement and it will lead you through all patterns and it will seem to you the master movement. But the seeming will be true. Let no mouth open to gainsay it. There seems no plan because it is all plan: there seems no centre because it is all centre. Blessed be He!'

Perelandra, ch. 17

Perfect goodness can never debate about the end to be attained, and perfect wisdom cannot debate about the means most suited to achieve it. The freedom of God consists in the fact that no cause other than Himself produces His acts and no external obstacle impedes them—that His own goodness is the root from which they all grow and His own omnipotence the air in which they all flower.

The Problem of Pain, ch. 2

Kingship and power and festal pomp and courtesy shot from him as sparks fly from an anvil. The pealing of bells, the blowing of trumpets, the spreading out of banners, are means used on earth to make a faint symbol of his quality. It was like a long sunlit wave, creamy-crested and arched with emerald, that comes on nine feet tall, with roaring and with terror and unquenchable laughter. It was like the first beginning of music in the halls of some King so high and at some festival so solemn that a tremor akin to fear runs through young hearts when they hear it. For this was great Glund-Oyarsa, King of Kings, through whom the joy of creation principally blows across these fields of Arbol, known to men in old times as Jove and under that name, by fatal but not inexplicable misprision, confused with his Maker—so little did they dream by how many degrees the stair even of created being rises above him.

That Hideous Strength, ch. 15

No philosophical theory which I have yet come across is a radical improvement on the words of *Genesis*, that 'In the beginning God made Heaven and Earth'.

Miracles, ch. 4

As our Earth is to all the stars, so doubtless are we men and our concerns to all creation; as all the stars are to space itself, so are all creatures, all thrones and powers and mightiest of the created gods, to the abyss of the self-existing Being, who is to us Father and Redeemer and indwelling Comforter, but of whom no man nor angel can say nor conceive what He is in and for Himself, or what is the work that he 'maketh from the beginning to the end'. For they are all derived and unsubstantial things. Their vision fails them and they cover their eyes from the intolerable light of utter actuality, which was and is and shall be, which never could have been otherwise, which has no opposite.

The Problem of Pain, ch. 10

Our prayers are granted, or not, in eternity. The task of dovetailing the spiritual and physical histories of the world into each other is accomplished in the total act of creation itself. Our prayers, and other free acts, are known to us only as we come to the moment of doing them. But they are eternally in the score of the great symphony. Not 'pre-determined'; the syllable *pre* lets in the notion of eternity as simply an older time. For though we cannot experience our life as an endless present, we are eternal in God's eyes; that is, in our deepest reality.

Letters to Malcolm, ch. 20

One of the purposes for which God instituted prayer may have been to bear witness that the course of events is not governed like a state but created like a work of art to which every being makes its own contribution and (in prayer) a conscious contribution, and in which every being is both an

end and a means. .... The world was made partly that there
might be prayer. .... But let's have finished with 'partly'. The
great work of art was made for the sake of all it does and is,
down to the curve of every wave and the flight of every
insect.

Letters to Malcolm, ch. 10

An ordinary simple Christian kneels down to say his prayers.
He is trying to get in touch with God. But if he is a Christian
he knows that what is prompting him to pray is also God: God,
so to speak, inside him. But he also knows that all his real
knowledge of God comes through Christ, the Man who was
God—that Christ is standing beside him, helping him to pray,
praying for him. You see what is happening. God is the thing
to which he is praying—the goal he is trying to reach. God is
also the thing inside him which is pushing him on—the motive
power. God is also the road or bridge along which he is being
pushed to that goal. So that the whole threefold life of the
three-personal Being is actually going on in that ordinary little
bedroom where an ordinary man is saying his prayers. The
man is being caught up into the higher kind of life—what I
called *Zoe* or spiritual life: he is being pulled into God, by God,
while still remaining himself.

Mere Christianity, bk 4, ch. 2

The good is uncreated; it never could have been otherwise;
it has no shadow of contingency; it lies, as Plato said, on the
other side of existence. It is the *Rita* of the Hindus by which the
gods themselves are divine, the *Tao* of the Chinese from which
all realities proceed, But we, favoured beyond the wisest
pagans, know what lies beyond existence, what admits no
contingency, what lends divinity to all else, what is the ground
of all existence, is not simply a law but also a begetting love, a
love begotten, and the love which, being between these two, is
also imminent in all those who are caught up to share the unity

of their self-caused life. God is not merely good, but goodness; goodness is not merely divine, but God.

'The Poison of Subjectivism', *Christian Reflections*

There were in the eighteenth century terrible theologians who held that 'God did not command certain things because they are right, but certain things are right because God commanded them'. To make the position perfectly clear, one of them even said that though God has, as it happens, commanded us to love Him and one another, He might equally well have commanded us to hate Him and one another, and hatred would then have been right. It was apparently a mere toss-up which He decided on. Such a view of course makes God a mere arbitrary tyrant. It would be better and less irreligious to believe in no God and to have no ethics than to have such an ethics and such a theology as this.

Reflections on the Psalms, ch. 6

When we merely *say* that we are bad, the 'wrath' of God seems a barbarous doctrine; as soon as we *perceive* our badness, it appears inevitable, a mere corollary from God's goodness.

The Problem of Pain, ch. 4

Anger—no peevish fit of temper, but just, generous, scalding indignation—passes (not necessarily at once) into embracing, exultant, re-welcoming love. That is how friends and lovers are truly reconciled. Hot wrath, hot love. Such anger is the fluid that love bleeds when you cut it. The *angers*, not the measured remonstrances, of lovers are love's renewal. Wrath and pardon are both, as applied to God, analogies; but they belong together to the same circle of analogy—the circle of life, and love, and deeply personal relationships. All the liberalising and 'civilising' analogies only lead us astray. Turn God's wrath into mere enlightened disapproval, and you also turn His love into mere humanitarianism. The 'consuming fire' and the 'perfect beauty' both vanish.

Letters to Malcolm, ch. 18

The Divine 'goodness' differs from ours, but it is not sheerly different: it differs from ours not as white from black but as a perfect circle from a child's first attempt to draw a wheel. But when the child has learned to draw, it will know that the circle it then makes is what it was trying to make from the very beginning.

This doctrine is presupposed in Scripture. Christ calls men to repent—a call which would be meaningless if God's standard were sheerly different from that which they already knew and failed to practise.

The Problem of Pain, ch. 3

Mercy, detached from Justice, grows unmerciful.

'The Humanitarian Theory of Punishment',
Res Judicatae (June 1953)

If the universe is not governed by an absolute goodness, then all our efforts are in the long run hopeless. But if it is, then we are making ourselves enemies to that goodness every day, and are not in the least likely to do any better tomorrow, and so our case is hopeless again. We cannot do without it, and we cannot do with it. God is the only comfort, He is also the supreme terror: the thing we most need and the thing we most want to hide from. He is our only possible ally, and we have made ourselves His enemies. Some people talk as if meeting the gaze of absolute goodness would be fun. They need to think again. They are still only playing with religion.

Mere Christianity, bk 1, ch. 5

To be sovereign of the universe is no great matter to God. . . . We must keep always before our eyes that vision of Lady

Julian's in which God carried in His hand a little object like a nut, and that nut was 'all that is made'. God, who needs nothing, loves into existence wholly superfluous creatures in order that He may love and perfect them.

The Four Loves, ch. 6

On the whole, God's love for us is a much safer subject to think about than our love for Him. Nobody can always have devout feelings: and even if we could, feelings are not what God principally cares about Christian Love, either towards God or towards man, is an affair of the will. If we are trying to do His will we are obeying the commandment, 'Thou shalt love the Lord thy God.' He will give us feelings of love if He pleases. We cannot create them for ourselves, and we must not demand them as a right. But the great thing to remember is that, though our feelings come and go, his love for us does not. It is not wearied by our sins, or our indifference; and, therefore, it is quite relentless in its determination that we shall be cured of those sins, at whatever cost to us, at whatever cost to Him.

Mere Christianity, bk 3, ch. 9

Pure, spiritual, intellectual love shot from their faces like barbed lightning. It was so unlike the love we experience that its expression could easily be mistaken for ferocity.

Perelandra, ch. 16

We want, in fact, not so much a Father in Heaven as a grandfather in heaven—a senile benevolence who, as they say, 'liked to see young people enjoying themselves' and whose plan for the universe was simply that it might be truly said at the end of each day, 'a good time was had by all'. . . .

It is for people whom we care nothing about that we demand happiness on any terms: with our friends, our lovers, our children, we are exacting and would rather see them suffer much than be happy in contemptible and estranging modes. If

God is Love, He is, by definition, something more than mere kindness. And it appears, from all the records, that though He has often rebuked us and condemned us, He has never regarded us with contempt. He has paid us the intolerable compliment of loving us, in the deepest, most tragic, most inexorable sense.

The Problem of Pain, ch. 3

We are, not metaphorically but in very truth, a Divine work of art, something that God is making, and therefore something with which He will not be satisfied until it has a certain character. Here again we come up against what I have called the 'intolerable compliment'. Over a sketch made idly to amuse a child, an artist may not take much trouble: he may be content to let it go even though it is not exactly as he meant it to be. But over the great picture of his life—the work which he loves, though in a different fashion, as intensely as a man loves a woman or a mother a child—he will take endless trouble—and would, doubtless, thereby *give* endless trouble to the picture if it were sentient. One can imagine a sentient picture, after being rubbed and scraped and re-commenced for the tenth time, wishing that it were only a thumb-nail sketch whose making was over in a minute. In the same way, it is natural for us to wish that God had designed for us a less glorious and less arduous destiny; but then we are wishing not for more love but for less.

Ibid.

In [the dog's] state of nature it has a smell, and habits, which frustrate man's love: he washes it, house-trains it, teaches it not to steal, and is so enabled to love it completely. To the puppy the whole proceeding would seem, if it were a theologian, to cast grave doubts on the 'goodness' of man: but the full-grown and full-trained dog, larger, healthier, and longer-lived than the wild dog, and admitted, as it were by Grace, to a whole world of affections, loyalties, interests, and comforts entirely beyond its animal destiny, would have no such doubts. . . . We may wish, indeed, that we were of so little account to God that He left us alone to follow our natural impulses—that He would give over trying to train us into something so unlike our natural selves: but once again, we are asking not for more Love, but for less.

Ibid.

When Christianity says that God loves man, it means that God *loves* man: not that He has some 'disinterested', because really indifferent, concern for our welfare, but that, in awful and surprising truth, we are the objects of His love. You asked for a loving God: you have one. The great spirit you so lightly invoked, the 'lord of terrible aspect', is present: not a senile benevolence that drowsily wishes you to be happy in your own way, not the cold philanthropy of a conscientious magistrate, nor the care of a host who feels responsible for the comfort of his guests, but the consuming fire Himself, the Love that made the worlds, persistent as the artist's love for his work and despotic as a man's love for a dog, provident and venerable as a father's love for a child, jealous, inexorable, exacting as love between the sexes.

Ibid.

The problem of reconciling human suffering with the existence of a God who loves, is only insoluble so long as we attach a trivial meaning to the word 'love', and look on things as if man were the centre of them. Man is not the centre. God does not exist for the sake of man. Man does not exist for his own sake. . . . To ask that God's love should be content with us as we are is to ask that God should cease to be God: because He is what He is, His love must, in the nature of things, be impeded and repelled, by certain stains in our present character, and because He already loves us He must labour to make us lovable. . . . What we would here and now call our 'happiness'

is not the end God chiefly has in view: but when we are such
as He can love without impediment, we shall in fact be happy.
                                                        Ibid.

If the world exists not chiefly that we may love God but that
God may love us, yet that very fact, on a deeper level, is so for
our sakes. If He who in Himself can lack nothing chooses to
need us, it is because we need to be needed. Before and behind
all the relations of God to man, as we now learn them from
Christianity, yawns the abyss of a Divine act of pure giving—
the election of man, from nonentity, to be the beloved of
God. . . .

Our highest activity must be response, not initiative. To
experience the love of God in a true, and not an illusory form,
is therefore to experience it as our surrender to His demand,
our conformity to His desire.   *Ibid.*

When we want to be something other than the thing God
wants us to be, we must be wanting what, in fact, will not
make us happy. Those Divine demands which sound to our
natural ears most like those of a despot and least like those of a
lover, in fact marshall us where we should want to go if we
knew what we wanted. He demands our worship, our obedience, our prostration. . . . A man can no more diminish God's
glory by refusing to worship Him than a lunatic can put out
the sun by scribbling the word 'darkness' on the walls of his
cell. But God wills our good, and our good is to love him. . . .

That is, whether we like it or not, God intends to give us
what we need, not what we now think we want. Once more,
we are embarrassed by the intolerable compliment, by too
much love, not too little. . . .

If we will not learn to eat the only food that the universe
grows—the only food that any possible universe ever can
grow—then we must starve eternally.

                                                        Ibid.

The passion of love is something that happens to us, as 'getting wet' happens to a body: and God is exempt from that 'passion' in the same way that water is exempt from 'getting wet'. He cannot be affected with love, because He *is* love. To imagine that love as something less torrential or less sharp than our own temporary and derivative 'passions' is a most disastrous fantasy.

Miracles, ch. 11

All sorts of people are fond of repeating the Christian statement that 'God is love'. But they seem not to notice that the words 'God is love' have no real meaning unless God contains at least two Persons. Love is something that one person has for another person. If God was a single person, then before the world was made, He was not love. Of course, what these people mean when they say that God is love is often something quite different: they really mean 'Love is God'. They really mean that our feelings of love, however and wherever they arise, and whatever results they produce, are to be treated with great respect. Perhaps they are: but that is something quite different from what Christians mean by the statement 'God is love'. They believe that the living, dynamic activity of love has been going on in God for ever and has created everything else.

Mere Christianity, bk 4, ch. 4

The essential attitude of Platonism is aspiration or longing: the human soul, imprisoned in the shadowy, unreal world of Nature, stretches out its hands and struggles towards the beauty and reality of that which lies (as Plato says) 'on the other side of existence'. . . . . In Christianity, however, the human soul is not the seeker but the sought: it is God who seeks, who descends from the other world to find and heal Man; the parable about the Good Shepherd looking for and finding the lost sheep sums it up.

Studies in Medieval and Renaissance Literature, ch. 9, sec. 3

Creation seems to be delegation through and through. He will do nothing simply by Himself which can be done by creatures. I suppose this is because He is a giver. And He has nothing to give but Himself. And to give Himself is to do His deeds—in a sense, and on varying levels to be Himself—through the things He has made.

Letters to Malcolm, ch. 13

Many of those who say they dislike Milton's God only mean that they dislike God: infinite sovereignty *de jure*, combined with infinite power *de facto*, and love which, by its very nature, includes wrath also—it is not only in poetry that these things offend. . . .

When we remember that we also have our places in this plot, that we also, at any given moment, are moving either towards the Messianic or towards the Satanic position, then we are entering the world of religion. But when we do that, our epic holiday is over: we rightly shut up our Milton.

A Preface to 'Paradise Lost', ch. 19

You will certainly carry out God's purpose, however you act, but it makes a difference to you whether you serve like Judas or like John.

The Problem of Pain, ch. 7

'He is all a burning joy and a strength. . . .
'How can I step out of His will save into something that cannot be wished?'

Perelandra, ch. 9

2. CHRIST

'Are you not thirsty?' said the Lion.
'I'm *dying* of thirst,' said Jill.

'Then drink,' said the Lion.

'May I—could I—would you mind going away while I do?' said Jill.

The Lion answered this only by a look and a very low growl. . . .

'I daren't come and drink,' said Jill.

'Then you will die of thirst,' said the Lion.

'Oh dear!' said Jill, coming another step nearer. 'I suppose I must go and look for another stream then.'

'There is no other stream,' said the Lion.

The Silver Chair, ch. 2

'Yes,' said Queen Lucy. 'In our world too, a Stable once had something inside it that was bigger than our whole world.'

The Last Battle, ch. 13

Then comes the real shock. Among these Jews there suddenly turns up a man who goes about talking as if He was God. He claims to forgive sins. He says He has always existed. He says He is coming to judge the world at the end of time. Now let us get this clear. Among Pantheists, like the Indians, anyone might say that he was a part of God, or one with God: there would be nothing very odd about it. But this man, since He was a Jew, could not mean that kind of God. God, in their language, meant the Being outside the world Who had made it and was infinitely different from anything else. And when you have grasped that, you will see that what this man said was, quite simply, the most shocking thing that has ever been uttered by human lips.

Mere Christianity, bk 2, ch. 3

There was a man born among these Jews who claimed to be, or to be the son of, or to be 'one with', the Something which is at once the awful haunter of nature and the giver of the moral law. The claim is so shocking—a paradox, and even a horror, which we may easily be lulled into taking too lightly—that only two views of this man are possible. Either he was a raving lunatic of an unusually abominable type, or else He was, and is, precisely what He said. There is no middle way. If the records make the first hypothesis unacceptable, you must submit to the second. And if you do that, all else that is claimed by Christians becomes credible.

The Problem of Pain, ch. 1

He says again 'I am the begotten of the One God, before Abraham was, I am,' and remember what the words 'I am' were in Hebrew. They were the name of God, which must not be spoken by any human being, the name which it was death to utter. . . .

If you had gone to Budda and asked him, 'Are you the son of Bramah?' he would have said, 'My son, you are still in the vale of illusion.' If you had gone to Socrates and asked, 'Are you Zeus?' he would have laughed at you. If you had gone to Mohammed and asked, 'Are you Allah?' he would first have rent his clothes and then cut your head off. If you had asked Confucius, 'Are you Heaven?' I think he would have probably replied, 'Remarks which are not in accordance with nature are in bad taste.' The idea of a great moral teacher saying what Christ said is out of the question. In my opinion, the only person who can say that sort of thing is either God or a complete lunatic suffering from that form of delusion which undermines the whole mind of man. . . . He was never regarded as a mere moral teacher. He did not produce that effect on any of the people who actually met Him. He produced mainly three effects—Hatred—Terror—Adoration. There was no trace of people expressing mild approval.

'What Are We to Make of Jesus Christ?'
Asking Them Questions

If anything whatever is common to all believers, and even

to many unbelievers, it is the sense that in the Gospels they have met a personality. . . . We are not in the least perturbed by the contrasts . . . in Jesus of peasant shrewdness, intolerable severity, and irresistible tenderness. So strong is the flavour of the personality that, even while He says things which, on any other assumption than that of Divine Incarnation in the fullest sense, would be appallingly arrogant, yet we—and many un-believers too—accept Him at His own valuation when He says, 'I am meek and lowly of heart.'

'Modern Theology and Biblical Criticism',
Christian Reflections

God could, had He pleased, have been incarnate in a man of iron nerves, the Stoic sort who lets no sigh escape him. Of His great humility He chose to be incarnate in a man of delicate sensibilities who wept at the grave of Lazarus and sweated blood in Gethsemane. Otherwise we should have missed the great lesson that it is by his *will* alone that a man is good or bad, and that *feelings* are not, in themselves, of any importance. We should also have missed the all-important help of knowing that He has faced all that the weakest of us face, has shared not only the strength of our nature but every weakness of it except sin. If He had been incarnate in a man of immense natural courage, that would have been for many of us almost the same as His not being incarnate at all.

Letters (c. October 1947)

'He dwells (all of Him dwells) within the seed of the smallest flower and is not cramped: Deep Heaven is inside Him who is inside the seed and does not distend Him. Blessed be He!' . . .

'Where Maleldil is, there is the centre. He is in every place. Not some of Him in one place and some in another, but in each place the whole Maleldil, even in the smallness beyond thought. There is no way out of the centre save into the Bent Will which cast itself into the Nowhere. Blessed be He!' . . .

'In His city all things are made for each. When He died in the Wounded World He died not for men, but for each man. If each man had been the only man made, He would have done no less. Each thing, from the single grain of Dust to the strongest eldil, is the end and the final cause of all creation and the mirror in which the beam of His brightness comes to rest and so returns to Him. Blessed be He!'

Perelandra, ch. 17

'Don't you mind him,' said Puddleglum. 'There *are* no accidents. Our guide is Aslan.'

The Silver Chair, ch. 10

If ever a myth had become fact, had been incarnated, it would be just like this. And nothing else in all literature was just like this. Myths were like it in one way. Histories were like it in another. But nothing was simply like it. And no person was like the Person it depicted; as real, as recognisable, through all that depth of time, as Plato's Socrates or Boswell's Johnson (ten times more so than Eckermann's Goethe or Lockhart's Scott), yet also numinous, lit by a light from beyond the world, a god. But if a god—we are no longer polytheists—then not a god, but God. Here and here only in all time the myth must have become fact; the Word, flesh; God, Man.

Surprised by Joy, ch. 15

'Is—is he a man?' asked Lucy.

'Aslan a man!' said Mr. Beaver sternly. 'Certainly not. I tell you he is the King of the wood and the son of the great Emperor-Beyond-the-Sea. Don't you know who is the King of Beasts? Aslan is a lion—*the* Lion, the great Lion.'

'Ooh!' said Susan, 'I'd thought he was a man. Is he—quite safe? I shall feel rather nervous about meeting a lion.'

'That you will, dearie, and no mistake,' said Mrs. Beaver, 'if there's anyone who can appear before Aslan without their knees knocking, they're either braver than most or else just silly.'

'Then he isn't safe?' said Lucy.

'Safe?' said Mr. Beaver. 'Don't you hear what Mrs. Beaver tells you? Who said anything about safe? 'Course he isn't safe. But he's good. He's the King, I tell you.'

The Lion, the Witch and the Wardrobe, ch. 8

I think all Christians would agree with me if I said that though Christianity seems at first to be all about morality, all about duties and rules and guilt and virtue, yet it leads you on, out of all that, into something beyond. One has a glimpse of a country where they do not talk of those things, except perhaps as a joke. Every one there is filled full with what we should call goodness as a mirror is filled with light. But they do not call it goodness. They do not call it anything. They are not thinking of it. They are too busy looking at the source from which it comes.

Mere Christianity, bk 3, ch. 12

No man knows how bad he is till he has tried very hard to be good. A silly idea is current that good people do not know what temptation means. This is an obvious lie. Only those who try to resist temptation know how strong it is. . . . You find out the strength of a wind by trying to walk against it, not by lying down. A man who gives in to temptation after five minutes simply does not know what it would have been like an hour later. That is why bad people, in one sense, know very little about badness. They have lived a sheltered life by always giving in. We never find out the strength of the evil impulse inside us until we try to fight it: and Christ, because He was the only man who never yielded to temptation, is also the only man who knows to the full what temptation means—the only complete realist.

Ibid., bk 3, ch. 11

'I'm ready to accept Jesus as a great moral teacher, but I don't accept His claim to be God.' That is the one thing we must not say. A man who was merely a man and said the sort of things Jesus said would not be a great moral teacher. He would either be a lunatic—on a level with the man who says he is a poached egg—or else he would be the Devil of Hell. You must make your choice. Either this man was, and is, the Son of God: or else a madman or something worse. You can shut Him up for a fool, you can spit at Him and kill Him as a demon; or you can fall at His feet and call Him Lord and God. But let us not come with any patronizing nonsense about His being a great human teacher. He has not left that open to us. He did not intend to.

Ibid., bk 2, ch. 3

We may observe that the teaching of Our Lord Himself, in which there is no imperfection, is not given us in that cut-and-dried, fool-proof, systematic fashion we might have expected or desired. He wrote no book. We have only reported sayings, most of them uttered in answer to questions, shaped in some degree by their context. And when we have collected them all we cannot reduce them to a system. He preaches but he does not lecture. He uses paradox, proverb, exaggeration, parable, irony; even (I mean no irreverence) the 'wisecrack'. He utters maxims which, like popular proverbs, if rigorously taken, may seem to contradict one another. His teaching therefore cannot be grasped by the intellect alone, cannot be 'got up' as if it were a 'subject'. If we try to do that with it, we shall find Him the most elusive of teachers. He hardly ever gave a straight answer to a straight question. He will not be, in the way we want, 'pinned down'. The attempt is (again, I mean no irreverence) like trying to bottle a sunbeam.

Reflections on the Psalms, ch. 11

Before his Mother had borne him, before his ancestors had been called Ransoms, before *ransom* had been the name for a payment that delivers, before the world was made, all these things had so stood together in eternity that the very significance of the pattern at this point lay in their coming together in just this fashion. And he bowed his head and groaned and repined against his fate—to be still a man and yet to be forced up into the metaphysical world, to enact what philosophy only thinks.

'My name also is Ransom,' said the Voice.

Perelandra, ch. 11

Did you ever think, when you were a child, what fun it would be if your toys could come to life? Well suppose you could really have brought them to life. Imagine turning a tin soldier into a real little man. It would involve turning the tin into flesh. And suppose the tin soldier did not like it. He is not interested in flesh; all he sees is that the tin is being spoilt. He thinks you are killing him. He will do everything he can to prevent you. He will not be made into a man if he can help it.

What you would have done about that tin soldier I do not know. But what God did about us was this. The Second Person in God, the Son, became human Himself: was born into the world as an actual man—a real man of a particular height, with hair of a particular colour, speaking a particular language, weighing so many stone. The Eternal Being, who knows everything and who created the whole universe, became not only a man but (before that) a baby, and before that a *foetus* inside a Woman's body. If you want to get the hang of it, think how you would like to become a slug or a crab.

The Man in Christ rose again: not only the God. That is the whole point. For the first time we saw a real man. One tin soldier—real tin, just like the rest—had come fully and splendidly alive.

Mere Christianity, bk 4, ch. 5

Now the truth is, I think, that the sweetly-attractive-human-Jesus is a product of 19th century scepticism, produced by people who were ceasing to believe in His divinity but wanted to keep as much Christianity as they could. It is not what an unbeliever coming to the records with an open mind will (at first) find there. The first thing you find is that we are simply not *invited* to speak, to pass any moral judgement on Him, however favourable; it is only too clear that He is going to do whatever judging there is; it is *we* who are *being* judged, sometimes tenderly, sometimes with stunning severity, but always *de haut en bas*.

Letters (26 March 1940)

'Welcome, child,' he said.
'Aslan,' said Lucy, 'you're bigger.'
'That is because you are older, little one,' answered he.
'Not because you are?'
'I am not. But every year you grow, you will find me bigger.'

Prince Caspian, ch. 10

He knew none of the true stories about Aslan, the great Lion, the son of the Emperor-over-sea, the King above all High Kings in Narnia. But after one glance at the Lion's face he slipped out of the saddle and fell at its feet. . . .
The High King above all kings stooped towards him. . . . He lifted his face and their eyes met. Then instantly the pale brightness of the mist and the fiery brightness of the Lion rolled themselves together into a swirling glory and gathered themselves up and disappeared.

The Horse and His Boy, ch. 11

The pure light walks the earth; the darkness, received into the heart of Deity, is there swallowed up. Where, except in uncreated light, can the darkness be drowned?

Letters to Malcolm, ch. 13

If God were a Kantian, who would not have us till we came
to Him from the purest and best motives, who could be saved?
The Problem of Pain, ch. 6

'Oh, Aslan,' said she, 'it was kind of you to come.'
'I have been here all the time,' said he, 'but you have just
made me visible.'
'Aslan!' said Lucy almost a little reproachfully. 'Don't make
fun of me. As if anything *I* could do would make *you*
visible!'
'It did,' said Aslan. 'Do you think I wouldn't obey my own
rules?'
The Voyage of the 'Dawn Treader', ch. 10

'Now Bree,' he said, 'you poor, proud, frightened Horse,
draw near. Nearer still, my son. Do not dare not to dare.
Touch me. Smell me. Here are my paws, here is my tail, these
are my whiskers. I am a true Beast.'
'Aslan,' said Bree in a shaken voice, 'I'm afraid I must be
rather a fool.'
'Happy the Horse who knows that while he is still young. Or
the Human either.'
The Horse and His Boy, ch. 14

In Gethsemane it is essential Freedom that is asked to be
bound, unwearied control to throw up the sponge, Life itself to
die. Ordinary men have not been so much in love with life as is
usually supposed: small as their share of it is, they have found it
too much to bear without reducing a large portion of it as
nearly to non-life as they can: we love drugs, sleep, irresponsi-
bility, amusement, are more than half in love with easeful
death—if only we could be sure it wouldn't hurt! Only He
who really lived a human life (and I presume that only one did)
can fully taste the horror of death.
Letters (c. September 1940)

People ate their dinners and felt better long before the theory of vitamins was ever heard of: and if the theory of vitamins is some day abandoned they will go on eating their dinners just the same. Theories about Christ's death are not Christianity: they are explanations about how it works. . . .

We are told that Christ was killed for us, that His death has washed out our sins, and that by dying He disabled death itself. That is the formula. That is Christianity. That is what has to be believed. Any theories we build up as to how Christ's death did all this are, in my view, quite secondary: mere plans or diagrams to be left alone if they do not help us, and, even if they do help us, not to be confused with the thing itself.

Mere Christianity, bk 2, ch. 4

'It means,' said Aslan, 'that though the Witch knew the Deep Magic, there is a magic deeper still which she did not know. Her knowledge goes back only to the dawn of Time. But if she could have looked a little further back, into the stillness and the darkness before Time dawned, she would have read there a different incantation. She would have known that when a willing victim who had committed no treachery was killed in a traitor's stead, the Table would crack and Death itself would start working backwards.'

The Lion, the Witch and the Wardrobe, ch. 15

Some people probably think of the Resurrection as a desperate last moment expedient to save the Hero from a situation which had got out of the Author's control.

Miracles, ch. 12

The idea which . . . shuts out the Second Coming from our minds, the idea of the world slowly ripening to perfection, is a myth, not a generalization from experience. And it is a myth which distracts us from our real duties and our real interest. It is our attempt to guess the plot of a drama in which we are the characters. But how can the characters in a play guess the plot? We are not the playwright, we are not the producer, we are not even the audience. We are on the stage. To play well the scenes in which we are 'on' concerns us much more than to guess about the scenes that follow it.

The World's Last Night, ch. 7

The doctrine of the Second Coming teaches us that we do not and cannot know when the world drama will end. The curtain may be rung down at any moment. ... This seems to some people intolerably frustrating. ... We do not know the play. ... The Author knows. The audience, if there is an audience (if angels and archangels and all the company of heaven fill the pit and the stalls) may have an inkling. ... When it is over, we may be told. We are led to expect that the Author will have something to say to each of us on the part that each of us has played. The playing it well is what matters infinitely.

Ibid.

Precisely because we cannot predict the moment, we must be ready at all moments. Our Lord repeated this practical conclusion again and again; as if the promise of the Return had been made for the sake of this conclusion alone. Watch, watch, is the burden of his advice. I shall come like a thief. You will not, I most solemnly assure you you will not, see me approaching. ... The point is surely simple enough. The schoolboy does not know which part of his Virgil lesson he will be made to translate: that is why he must be prepared to translate *any* passage. The sentry does not know at what time an enemy will attack, or an officer inspect, his post; that is why he must keep awake *all* the time. ...

Women sometimes have the problem of trying to judge by artificial light how a dress will look by daylight. That is very like the problem of all of us to dress our souls not for the electric lights of the present world but for the daylight of the next. The good dress is the one that will face that light. For that light will last longer.

Ibid.

3. THE HOLY SPIRIT AND ANGELS

Accept these sensations with thankfulness as birthday cards from God, but remember that they are only greetings, not the real gift. . . . The real thing is the gift of the Holy Spirit which can't usually be—perhaps not ever—experienced as a sensation or emotion. The sensations are merely the response of your nervous system. Don't depend on them. Otherwise when they go and you are once more emotionally flat (as you certainly will be quite soon), you might think that the real thing had gone too. But it won't. It will be there when you can't feel it. May even be most operative when you can feel it least.

Letters (15 May 1952)

Ordinarily, to be known by God is to be, for this purpose, in the category of things. We are like earthworms, cabbages, and nebulae, objects of divine knowledge. But when we (a) become aware of the fact— the present fact, not the generalisation—and (b) assent with all our will to be so known, then we treat ourselves, in relation to God, not as things but as persons. We have unveiled. Not that any veil could have baffled this sight. The change is in us. The passive changes to the active. Instead of merely being known, we show, we tell, we offer ourselves to view.

To put ourselves thus on a personal footing with God could, in itself and without warrant, be nothing but presumption and illusion. But we are taught that it is not; that it is God who gives us that footing. For it is by the Holy Spirit that we cry 'Father'. By unveiling, by confessing our sins and 'making

known' our requests, we assume the high rank of persons before Him. And He, descending, becomes a Person to us.

Letters to Malcolm, ch. 4

Long ago, before we were married, [Helen] was haunted all
one morning as she went about her work with the obscure sense
of God (so to speak) 'at her elbow', demanding her attention.
And of course, not being a perfected saint, she had the feeling
that it would be a question, as it usually is, of some unrepented
sin or tedious duty. At last she gave in—I know how one puts it
off—and faced Him. But the message was, 'I want to *give* you
something' and instantly she entered into joy.

A Grief Observed, ch. 3

'The angels,' he said, 'have no senses; their experience is
purely intellectual and spiritual. That is why we know something about God which they don't. There are particular aspects
of His love and joy which can be communicated to a created
being only by sensuous experience. Something of God which
the Seraphim can never quite understand flows into us from the
blue of the sky, the taste of honey, the delicious embrace of
water whether cold or hot, and even from sleep itself.'

'Scraps', *St James' Magazine* (December 1945)

'We do not truly see light, we only see slower things lit by it,
so that for us light is on the edge—the last thing we know before
things become too swift for us. But the body of an *eldil* is a
movement swift as light; you may say its body is made of light,
but not of that which is light for the *eldil*. His "light" is a
swifter movement which for us is nothing at all; and what we
call light is for him a thing like water, a visible thing, a thing he
can touch and bathe in—even a dark thing when not illumined
by the swifter. And what we call firm things—flesh and earth—
seem to him thinner, and harder to see, than our light, and more

like clouds, and nearly nothing. To us the *eldil* is a thin, half-real body that can go through walls and rocks: to himself he goes through them because he is solid and firm and they are like cloud. And what is true light to him and fills the heaven, so that he will plunge into the rays of the sun to refresh himself from it, is to us the black nothing in the sky at night. These things are not strange, Small One, though they are beyond our senses.'

Out of the Silent Planet, ch. 15

V

SIN

1. EVIL

'The story is not quite so simple as that,' said the old woman, 'so many things happened after the eating of the apple. For one thing, the taste created such a craving in the man and the woman that they thought they could never eat enough of it; and they were not content with all the wild apple trees, but planted more and more, and grafted mountain-apple on to every other kind of tree so that every fruit should have a dash of that taste in it. They succeeded so well that the whole vegetable system of the country is now infected: and there is hardly a fruit or a root in the land . . . that has not a little mountain-apple in it. You have never tasted anything that was quite free from it.'

The Pilgrim's Regress, bk 5, ch. 3

A creature revolting against a creator is revolting against the source of his own powers—including even his power to revolt. . . . It is like the scent of a flower trying to destroy the flower.

A Preface to 'Paradise Lost', ch. 13

Really, a young Atheist cannot guard his faith too carefully. Dangers lie in wait for him on every side. You must not do, you must not even try to do, the will of the Father unless you are prepared to 'know of the doctrine'. All my acts, desires, and thoughts were to be brought into harmony with universal

Spirit. For the first time I examined myself with a seriously practical purpose. And there I found what appalled me; a zoo of lusts, a bedlam of ambitions, a nursery of fears, a harem of fondled hatreds. My name was legion.

Surprised by Joy, ch. 14

Is it still God speaking when a liar or a blasphemer speaks? In one sense, almost Yes. Apart from God he could not speak at all; there are no words not derived from the Word; no acts not derived from Him who is *Actus purus*. And indeed the only way in which I can make real to myself what theology teaches about the heinousness of sin is to remember that every sin is the distortion of an energy breathed into us—an energy which, if not thus distorted, would have blossomed into one of those holy acts whereof 'God did it' and 'I did it' are both true descriptions. We poison the wine as He decants it into us; murder a melody He would play with us as the instrument. We caricature the self-portrait He would paint. Hence all sin, whatever else it is, is sacrilege.

Letters to Malcolm, ch. 13

We have a strange illusion that mere time cancels sin. I have heard others, and I have heard myself, recounting cruelties and falsehoods committed in boyhood as if they were no concern of the present speaker's, and even with laughter. But mere time does nothing either to the fact or to the guilt of a sin. The guilt is washed out not by time but by repentance and the blood of Christ.

The Problem of Pain, ch. 4

This was the first thing Mark had been asked to do which he himself, before he did it, clearly knew to be criminal. But the moment of his consent almost escaped his notice; certainly, there was no struggle, no sense of turning a corner. There may have been a time in the world's history when such moments fully revealed their gravity, with witches prophesying on a blasted heath or visible Rubicons to be crossed. But, for him, it all slipped past in a chatter of laughter, of that intimate laughter between fellow professionals, which of all earthly powers is strongest to make men do very bad things before they are yet, individually, very bad men.

That Hideous Strength, ch. 6

And then she understood the devilish cunning of the enemies' plan. By mixing a little truth with it they had made their lie far stronger.

The Last Battle, ch. 9

Satan [in *Paradise Lost*] is the best drawn of Milton's characters. . . . The Satan in Milton enables him to draw the character well just as the Satan in us enables us to receive it. Not as Milton, but as man, he has trodden the burning marl, pursued vain war with heaven, and turned aside with leer malign. A fallen man *is* very like a fallen angel. . . . It is therefore right to say that Milton has put much of himself into Satan; but it is unwarrantable to conclude that he was pleased with that part of himself or expected us to be pleased. Because he was, like the rest of us, damnable, it does not follow that he was, like Satan, damned.

A Preface to 'Paradise Lost', ch. 13

To admire Satan [in *Paradise Lost*] is to give one's vote not only for a world of misery, but also for a world of lies and propaganda, of wishful thinking, of incessant autobiography. Yet the choice is possible. Hardly a day passes without some slight movement towards it in each one of us.

Ibid.

We have all often spoken—Ransom himself had often spoken —of a devilish smile. Now he realised that he had never taken the words seriously. The smile was not bitter, nor raging, nor, in an ordinary sense, sinister; it was not even mocking. It seemed to summon Ransom, with a horrible naiveté of welcome, into the world of its own pleasures, as if all men were at one in those pleasures, as if they were the most natural thing in the world and no dispute could ever have occurred about them. It was not furtive, nor ashamed, it had nothing of the conspirator in it. It did not defy goodness, it ignored it to the point of annihilation. Ransom perceived that he had never before seen anything but half-hearted and uneasy attempts at evil. This creature was whole-hearted. The extremity of its evil had passed beyond all struggle into some state which bore a horrible similarity to innocence. . . .

It came into his mind that in certain old philosophers and poets he had read that the mere sight of the devils was one of the greatest among the torments of Hell.

Perelandra, ch. 9

Hatred obscures all distinctions.

'On Science Fiction', *Of Other Worlds*

He had turned into a dragon while he was asleep. Sleeping on a dragon's hoard with greedy, dragonish thoughts in his heart, he had become a dragon himself.

The Voyage of the 'Dawn Treader', ch. 6

The whole point about Adam and Eve is that, as they would never, but for sin, have been old, so they were never young, never immature or undeveloped. They were created full-grown and perfect. . . . It is *we* who would have been the stammering boys, shifting uneasily from one foot to the other, red in the face, and hoping that our clownishness would be excused by our ignorance.

A Preface to 'Paradise Lost', ch. 16

'Don't you see,' said Straik, 'that we are offering you the unspeakable glory of being present at the creation of God Almighty? Here, in this house, you shall meet the first sketch of the real God. It is a man—or a being made by man—who will finally ascend the throne of the universe. And rule forever.'

That Hideous Strength, ch. 8

2. SELF

We try, when we wake, to lay the new day at God's feet; before we have finished shaving, it becomes *our* day and God's share in it is felt as a tribute which we must pay out of 'our own' pocket, a deduction from the time which ought, we feel, to be 'our own'. . . . A lover, in obedience to a quite uncalculating impulse, which may be full of good will as well as of desire and need not be forgetful of God, embraces his beloved, and then, quite innocently, experiences a thrill of sexual pleasure; but the second embrace may have that pleasure in view, may be a means to an end, may be the first downward step towards the state of regarding a fellow creature as a thing, as a machine to be used for his pleasure. Thus the bloom of innocence, the element of obedience and the readiness to take what comes is rubbed off every activity. . . . Thus all day long, and all the days of our life, we are sliding, slipping, falling away—as if God were, to our present consciousness, a smooth inclined plane on which there is no resting. . . . But God cannot have made us so. The gravitation away from God, 'the journey homeward to habitual self', must, we think, be a product of the Fall.

The Problem of Pain, ch. 5

What Satan put into the heads of our remote ancestors was the idea that they could 'be like gods'—could set up on their own as if they had created themselves—be their own masters—invent some sort of happiness for themselves outside God, apart from God. And out of that hopeless attempt has come nearly all that we call human history—money, poverty, ambition, war, prostitution, classes, empires, slavery—the long terrible story of man trying to find something other than God which will make him happy.

Mere Christianity, bk 2, ch. 3

Every story of conversion is the story of a blessed defeat.

Foreword to Joy Davidman's *Smoke on the Mountain*

The natural life in each of us is something self-centred, something that wants to be petted and admired, to take advantage of other lives, to exploit the whole universe. And especially it wants to be left to itself: to keep well away from anything better or stronger or higher than it, anything that might make it feel small. It is afraid of the light and air of the spiritual world, just as people who have been brought up to be dirty are afraid of a bath. And in a sense it is quite right. It knows that if the spiritual life gets hold of it, all its self-centredness and self-will are going to be killed and it is ready to fight tooth and nail to avoid that.

Mere Christianity, bk 4, ch. 5

Lord that made the dragon, grant me thy peace,
But say not that I should give up the gold,
Nor move, nor die. Others would have the gold.
Kill rather, Lord, the Men and the other dragons;
Then I can sleep; go when I will to drink.

'The Dragon Speaks', *Poems*

This act of self-will on the part of the creature, which constitutes an utter falseness to its true creaturely position, is the only sin that can be conceived as the Fall. For the difficulty about the first sin is that it must be very heinous, or its consequences would not be so terrible, and yet it must be something which a being free from the temptations of fallen man could conceivably have committed. The turning from God to self fulfills both conditions.

The Problem of Pain, ch. 5

The essence of religion, in my view, is the thirst for an end higher than natural ends; the finite self's desire for, and acquiescence in, and self-rejection in favour of, an object wholly good and wholly good for it. That the self-rejection will turn out to be also a self-finding, that bread cast upon the waters will be found after many days, that to die is to live—these are sacred paradoxes of which the human race must not be told too soon.

'A Christian Reply to Professor Price',
Phoenix Quarterly (Autumn 1946)

From the moment a creature becomes aware of God as God and of itself as self, the terrible alternative of choosing God or self for the centre is opened to it. This sin is committed daily by young children and ignorant peasants as well as by sophisticated persons, by solitaries no less than by those who live in society: it is the fall in every individual life, and in each day of each individual life, the basic sin behind all particular sins: at this very moment you and I are either committing it, or about to commit it, or repenting it.

The Problem of Pain, ch. 5

I would pay any price to be able to say truthfully 'All will be saved'. But my reason retorts, 'Without their will, or with it?' If I say 'Without their will' I at once perceive a contradiction; how can the supreme voluntary act of self-surrender be involuntary? If I say 'With their will', my reason replies 'How if they *will not* give in?'

Ibid., ch. 8

The dangers of apparent self-sufficiency explain why Our Lord regards the vices of the feckless and dissipated so much more leniently than the vices that lead to worldly success. Prostitutes are in no danger of finding their present life so satisfactory that they cannot turn to God: the proud, the avaricious, the self-righteous, are in that danger.

Ibid., ch. 6

The terrible thing, the almost impossible thing, is to hand over your whole self—all your wishes and precautions—to Christ. But it is far easier than what we are all trying to do instead. For what we are trying to do is to remain what we call 'ourselves', to keep personal happiness as our great aim in life, and yet at the same time be 'good'. We are all trying to let our mind and heart go their own way—centred on money or pleasure or ambition—and hoping, in spite of this, to behave honestly and chastely and humbly. And that is exactly what Christ warned us you could not do. As He said, a thistle cannot produce figs. If I am a field that contains nothing but grass-seed, I cannot produce wheat. Cutting the grass may keep it short: but I shall still produce grass and no wheat. If I want to produce wheat, the change must go deeper than the surface. I must be ploughed up and re-sown.

Mere Christianity, bk 4, ch. 8

The golden apple of selfhood, thrown among the false gods, became an apple of discord because they scrambled for it. They did not know the first rule of the holy game, which is that every player must by all means touch the ball and then immediately pass it on. To be found with it in your hands is a fault: to cling to it, death. But when it flies to and fro among the players too swift for eye to follow, the great master Himself leads the revelry, giving Himself eternally to His creatures in the generation, and back to Himself in the sacrifice, of the Word, then indeed the eternal dance 'makes heaven drowsy with the harmony.' . . . There is joy in the dance, but it does not exist for the sake of joy. It does not even exist for the sake of good, or of love. It is Love Himself and Good Himself, and therefore happy. It does not exist for us, but we for it.

The Problem of Pain, ch. 10

'Nothing, not even what is lowest and most bestial, will not be raised again if it submits to death.'

The Great Divorce, ch. 11

And as to God, we must remember that the soul is but a hollow which God fills. Its union with God is, almost by definition, a continual self-abandonment—an opening, an unveiling, a surrender, of itself. A blessed spirit is a mould ever more and more patient of the bright metal poured into it, a body ever more completely uncovered to the meridian blaze of the spiritual sun.

The Problem of Pain, ch. 10

For in self-giving, if anywhere, we touch a rhythm not only of all creation but of all being. For the Eternal Word also gives Himself in sacrifice; and that not only on Calvary. . . . From before the foundation of the world He surrenders begotten Deity back to begetting Deity in obedience. . . . From the highest to the lowest, self exists to be abdicated and, by that abdication, becomes the more truly self, to be thereupon yet the more abdicated, and so forever. This is not a heavenly law which we can escape by remaining earthly, nor an earthly law which we can escape by being saved. What is outside the system of self-giving is not earth, nor nature, nor 'ordinary life', but simply and solely Hell. Yet even Hell derives from this law such reality as it has. That fierce imprisonment in the self is but the obverse of the self-giving which is absolute reality; the negative shape which the outer darkness takes by surrounding and defining the shape of the real, or which the real imposes

on the darkness by having a shape and positive nature of its
own.

Ibid.

One of the happiest men and most pleasing companions I
have ever known was intensely selfish. On the other hand I
have known people capable of real sacrifice whose lives were
nevertheless a misery to themselves and to others, because self-
concern and self-pity filled all their thoughts. Either condition
will destroy the soul in the end. But till the end, give me the
man who takes the best of everything (even at my expense)
and then talks of other things, rather than the man who serves
me and talks of himself, and whose very kindnesses are a
continual reproach, a continual demand for pity, gratitude,
and admiration.

Surprised by Joy, ch. **9**

You are told to love your neighbour as yourself. How do
you love yourself? When I look into my own mind, I find that
I do not love myself by thinking myself a dear old chap or
having affectionate feelings. I do not think that I love myself
because I am particularly good, but just because I am myself
and quite apart from my character. . . . You dislike what you
have done, but you don't cease to love yourself. . . .

You may even think that you ought to go to the Police and
own up and be hanged. Love is not affectionate feeling, but a
steady wish for the loved person's ultimate good as far as it can
be obtained.

Answers to Questions on Christianity

In love we escape from our self into one other. In the moral
sphere, every act of justice or charity involves putting ourselves in the other person's place and thus transcending our own
competitive particularity. In coming to understand anything
we are rejecting the facts as they are for us in favour of the

facts as they are. The primary impulse of each is to maintain and aggrandise himself. The secondary impulse is to go out of the self, to correct its provincialism and heal its loneliness. In love, in virtue, in the pursuit of knowledge, and in the reception of the arts, we are doing this. Obviously this process can be described either as an enlargement or as a temporary annihilation of the self. But that is an old paradox; 'he that loseth his life shall save it'.

An Experiment in Criticism, Epilogue

3. PRIDE

There is one vice of which no man in the world is free; which every one in the world loathes when he sees it in someone else; and of which hardly any people, except Christians, ever imagine that they are guilty themselves. . . .

The essential vice, the utmost evil, is Pride. Unchastity, anger, greed, drunkenness, and all that, are mere fleabites in comparison: it was through Pride that the devil became the devil: Pride leads to every other vice: it is the complete anti-God state of mind. . . .

If I am a proud man, then, as long as there is one man in the whole world more powerful, or richer, or cleverer than I, he is my rival and my enemy. . . .

As long as you are proud you cannot know God. A proud man is always looking down on things and people: and, of course, as long as you are looking down, you cannot see something that is above you. . . .

The real test of being in the presence of God is that you either forget about yourself altogether or see yourself as a small, dirty object. It is better to forget about yourself altogether.

Mere Christianity, bk 3, ch. 8

The other, and less bad, vices come from the devil working on us through our animal nature. But [Pride] does not come through our animal nature at all. It comes direct from Hell. It is purely spiritual: consequently it is far more subtle and deadly. For the same reason, Pride can often be used to beat down the simpler vices. Teachers, in fact, often appeal to a boy's Pride, or, as they call it, his self-respect, to make him behave decently: many a man has overcome cowardice, or lust, or ill-temper by learning to think that they are beneath his dignity—that is, by Pride. The devil laughs. He is perfectly content to see you becoming chaste and brave and self-controlled provided, all the time, he is setting up in you the Dictatorship of Pride—just as he would be quite content to see your chilblains cured if he was allowed, in return, to give you cancer. For Pride is spiritual cancer: it eats up the very possibility of love, or contentment, or even common sense.

Ibid.

We next offer our own humility to God's admiration. Surely He'll like *that*? Or if not that, our clear-sighted and humble recognition that we still lack humility. Thus, depth beneath depth and subtlety within subtlety, there remains some lingering idea of our own, our very own, attractiveness. It is easy to acknowledge, but almost impossible to realise for long, that we are mirrors whose brightness, if we are bright, is wholly derived from the sun that shines upon us. Surely we must have a little—however little—native luminosity?

The Four Loves, ch. 6

No sooner do we believe that God loves us than there is an impulse to believe that He does so, not because He is Love, but because we are intrinsically lovable. The Pagans obeyed this impulse unabashed; a good man was 'dear to the gods' because he was good. We, being better taught, resort to subterfuge. Far be it from us to think that we have virtues for which God could love us. But then, how magnificently we have repented. As Bunyan says, describing his first and illusory conversion, 'I thought there was no man in England that pleased God better than I.'

Ibid.

> From all my lame defeats and oh! much more
> From all the victories that I seemed to score;
> From cleverness shot forth on Thy behalf
> At which, while angels weep, the audience laugh;
> From all my proofs of Thy divinity,
> Thou, who wouldst give no sign, deliver me. . . .
> Lord of the narrow gate and the needle's eye,
> Take from me all my trumpery lest I die.

'The Apologist's Evening Prayer', *Poems*

'Lead us not into temptation' often means, among other things, 'Deny me those gratifying invitations, those highly interesting contacts, that participation in the brilliant movements of our age, which I so often, at such risk, desire.'

Reflections on the Psalms, ch. 7

The man who truly and disinterestedly enjoys any one thing in the world, for its own sake, and without caring twopence what other people say about it, is by that very fact fore-armed against some of our subtlest modes of attack. You should always try to make the patient abandon the people or food or books he really likes in favour of the 'best' people, the 'right' food, the 'important' books.

The Screwtape Letters, ch. 13

A man is never so proud as when striking an attitude of humility.

'Christianity and Culture', *Christian Reflections*

When race is separated from race 'and grace prized in schism', when all our pleasure is to be *inside* some partial and arbitrary group, then of course, we must have 'outsiders' to despise and denounce—Jews, Capitalists, Papists, the Bourgeoisie, what-not—or it is no fun. That is how 'the primal curse' appears on the political level.

Arthurian Torso, pt 2, ch. 5

The niceness, in fact, is God's gift to Dick, not Dick's gift to God. . . .

A world of nice people, content in their own niceness, looking no further, turned away from God, would be just as desperately in need of salvation as a miserable world—and might even be more difficult to save.

Mere Christianity, bk 4, ch. 10

The pleasure of pride is like the pleasure of scratching. If there is an itch one does want to scratch; but it is much nicer to have *neither* the itch nor the scratch. As long as we have the itch of self-regard we shall want the pleasure of self-approval; but the happiest moments are those when we forget our precious selves and have neither but have everything else (God, our fellow humans, animals, the garden and the sky) instead.

Letters (18 February 1954)

VI

THE CHRISTIAN COMMITMENT

1. ALTERNATIVES

Your bid—for God or no God, for a good God or the Cosmic Sadist, for eternal life or nonentity—will not be serious if nothing much is staked on it. And you will never discover how serious it was until the stakes are raised horribly high; until you find that you are playing not for counters or for sixpences but for every penny you have in the world.

A Grief Observed, ch. 3

In the long run either Our Father or the Enemy will say 'Mine' of each thing that exists, and specially of each man.

The Screwtape Letters, ch. 21

As there is one Face above all worlds merely to see which is irrevocable joy, so at the bottom of all worlds that face is waiting whose sight alone is the misery from which none who beholds it can recover. And though there seemed to be, and indeed were, a thousand roads by which a man could walk through the world, there was not a single one which did not lead sooner or later either to the Beatific or the Miserific Vision.

Perelandra, ch. 9

Honest rejection of Christ, however mistaken, will be forgiven and healed—'whosoever shall speak a word against the

Son of Man, it shall be forgiven him.' But to *evade* the Son of Man; to look the other way; to pretend you haven't noticed; to become suddenly absorbed in something on the other side of the street; to leave the receiver off the telephone because it might be He who was ringing up; to leave unopened certain letters in a strange handwriting because they might be from Him—this is a different matter. You may not be certain yet whether you ought to be a Christian; but you do know you ought to be a Man, not an ostrich hiding its head in the sands.

Man or Rabbit?

'There is but one good; that is God. Everything else is good when it looks to Him and bad when it turns from Him. And the higher and mightier it is in the natural order, the more demoniac it will be if it rebels. It's not out of bad mice or bad fleas you make demons, but out of bad archangels. The false religion of lust is baser than the false religion of mother-love or patriotism or art: but lust is less likely to be made into a religion.'

The Great Divorce, ch. 11

I think we must fully face the fact that when Christianity does not make a man very much better, it makes him very much worse. It is, paradoxically, dangerous to draw nearer to God.

Letters (20 December 1961)

Those who will not be God's sons become His tools.

A Preface to 'Paradise Lost', ch. 10

'We have been on a fool's errand, then,' said John, 'ever since we left the main road.'

The Pilgrim's Regress, bk 6, ch. 5

Virtue—even attempted virtue—brings light; indulgence brings fog.

Mere Christianity, bk 3, ch. 5

When a man is getting better he understands more and more clearly the evil that is still left in him. When a man is getting worse, he understands his own badness less and less. A moderately bad man knows he is not very good: a thoroughly bad man thinks he is all right. This is common sense, really. You understand sleep when you are awake, not while you are sleeping. You can see mistakes in arithmetic when your mind is working properly: while you are making them you cannot see them. You can understand the nature of drunkenness when you are sober, not when you are drunk. Good people know about both good and evil: bad people do not know about either.

Ibid., bk 3, ch. 4

As one of the humans has said, active habits are strengthened by repetition but passive ones are weakened. The more often he feels without acting, the less he will be able ever to act, and, in the long run, the less he will be able to feel.

The Screwtape Letters, ch. 13

And the longer and more beautifully the Lion sang the harder Uncle Andrew tried to make himself believe that he could hear nothing but roaring. Now the trouble about trying to make yourself stupider than you really are is that you very often succeed. Uncle Andrew did. He soon did hear nothing but roaring in Aslan's song. Soon he couldn't have heard anything else even if he had wanted to.

The Magician's Nephew, ch. 10

If Christianity is untrue, then no honest man will want to believe it, however helpful it might be: if it is true, every honest man will want to believe it, even if it gives him no help at all.

Man or Rabbit?

'I saw that for years my life had been lived in two halves, never fitted together.'

Till We Have Faces, bk 1, ch. 13

Man approaches God most nearly when he is in one sense least like God. For what can be more unlike than fullness and need, sovereignty and humility, righteousness and penitence, limitless power and a cry for help?

The Four Loves, ch. 1

We must insist that dread and awe are in a different dimension from fear. They are in the nature of an interpretation man gives to the universe, or an impression he gets from it; and just as no enumeration of the physical qualities of a beautiful object could ever include its beauty, or give the faintest hint of what we mean by beauty to a creature without aesthetic experience, so no factual description of any human environment could include the uncanny and the Numinous or even hint at them. There seem, in fact, to be only two views we can hold about awe. Either it is a mere twist in the human mind, corresponding to nothing objective and serving no biological function, yet showing no tendency to disappear from that mind at its fullest development in poet, philosopher, or saint: or else it is a direct experience of the really supernatural, to which the name Revelation might properly be given.

The Problem of Pain, ch. 1

When the author walks on to the stage the play is over. God is going to invade, all right: but what is the good of saying you are on His side then, when you see the whole natural universe melting away like a dream and something else—something it never entered your head to conceive—comes crashing in; something so beautiful to some of us and so terrible to others that none of us will have any choice left? For this time it will be God without disguise; something so overwhelming that it will strike either irresistible love or irresistible horror into every creature. It will be too late then to choose your side. There is no use saying you choose to lie down when it has become impossible to stand up. That will not be the time for choosing: it will be the time when we discover which side we really have chosen, whether we realised it before or not. Now, today, this moment, is our chance to choose the right side.

Mere Christianity, bk 2, ch. 5

'No natural feelings are high or low, holy or unholy, in themselves. They are all holy when God's hand is on the rein. They all go bad when they set up on their own and make themselves into false gods.'

The Great Divorce, ch. 11

The idea of reaching 'a good life' without Christ is based on a double error. Firstly, we cannot do it; and secondly, in setting up 'a good life' as our final goal, we have missed the very point of our existence. Morality is a mountain which we cannot climb by our own efforts; and if we could we should only perish in the ice and the unbreathable air of the summit, lacking those wings with which the rest of the journey has to be accomplished. For it is *from* there that the real ascent begins. The ropes and axes are 'done away' and the rest is a matter of flying.

Man or Rabbit?

If you continue to love Jesus, nothing much can go wrong with you, and I hope you may always do so.

Unpublished letter to a little girl (26 October 1963)

2. THE NATURE OF CHRISTIANITY

How should man live save as glass
To let the white light without flame, the Father, pass
Unstained.

'Wormwood', Poems

For we are so little reconciled to time that we are even astonished at it. 'How he's grown!' we exclaim, 'How time flies!' as though the universal form of our experience were again and again a novelty. It is as strange as if a fish were repeatedly surprised at the wetness of water. And that would be strange indeed; unless of course the fish were destined to become, one day, a land animal.

Reflections on the Psalms, cn. 12

To make an organism which is also a spirit; to make that terrible oxymoron, a 'spiritual animal'. To take a poor primate, a beast with nerve-endings all over it, a creature with a stomach that wants to be filled, a breeding animal that wants its mate, and say, 'now get on with it. Become a god.'

A Grief Observed, ch. 4

God is no fonder of intellectual slackers than of any other slackers. If you are thinking of becoming a Christian, I warn you you are embarking on something which is going to take the whole of you, brains and all. But, fortunately, it works the other way round. Anyone who is honestly trying to be a Christian will soon find his intelligence being sharpened: one of the reasons why it needs no special education to be a Christian is that Christianity is an education itself. That is why an uneducated believer like Bunyan was able to write a book that has astonished the whole world.

Mere Christianity, bk 3, ch. 2

It is a serious thing to live in a society of possible gods and goddesses, to remember that the dullest and most uninteresting person you talk to may one day be a creature which, if you saw it now, you would be strongly tempted to worship, or else a horror and a corruption such as you now meet, if at all, only in a nightmare. . . . You have never talked to a mere mortal. Nations, cultures, arts, civilization—these are mortal, and their life is to ours as the life of a gnat. But it is immortals whom we joke with, work with, marry, snub, and exploit— immortal horrors or everlasting splendours. This does not mean that we are to be perpetually solemn. We must play. But our merriment must be of that kind (and it is, in fact, the merriest kind) which exists between people who have, from the outset, taken each other seriously—no flippancy, no superiority, no presumption. And our charity must be a real and costly love, with deep feeling for the sins in spite of which we love the sinner—no mere tolerance or indulgence which parodies love as flippancy parodies merriment. Next to the Blessed Sacrament itself, your neighbour is the holiest object presented to your senses. If he is your Christian neighbour he is holy in almost the same way, for in him also Christ *vere latitat*—the glorifier and the glorified, Glory Himself, is truly hidden.

Transposition and Other Addresses, ch. 2

The people who keep on asking if they can't lead a decent life without Christ, don't know what life is about; if they did they would know that 'a decent life' is mere machinery compared with the thing we men are really made for. Morality is indispensable; but the Divine Life, which gives itself to us and which calls us to be gods, intends for us something in which morality will be swallowed up. We are to be re-made. All the rabbit in us is to disappear—the worried, conscientious, ethical rabbit as well as the cowardly and sensual rabbit. We shall bleed and squeal as the handfuls of fur come out; and then, surprisingly, we shall find underneath it all a thing we have never yet imagined: a real Man, an ageless god, a son of God, strong, radiant, wise, beautiful, and drenched in joy.

Man or Rabbit?

'Look at me, now,' said the Ghost, slapping its chest (but the slap made no noise). 'I gone straight all my life. I don't say I was a religious man and I don't say I had no faults, far from it. But I done my best all my life, see? I done my best by everyone, that's the sort of chap I was. I never asked for anything that wasn't mine by rights. If I wanted a drink I paid for it and if I took my wages I done my job, see? That's the sort I was and I don't care who knows it. . . . But I got to have my rights same as you, see?'

'Oh no. It's not so bad as that. I haven't got my rights, or I should not be here. You will not get yours either. You'll get something far better. Never fear.'

'That's just what I say. I haven't got my rights. I always done my best and I never done nothing wrong. And what I don't see is why I should be put below a bloody murderer like you.'

'Who knows whether you will be? Only be happy and come with me.'

'What do you keep on arguing for? I'm only telling you the sort of chap I am. I only want my rights. I'm not asking for anybody's bleeding charity.'

'Then do. At once. Ask for the Bleeding Charity. Everything is here for the asking and nothing can be bought.'

The Great Divorce, ch. 4

God provides not for an abstraction called Man but for individual souls.

Letters (16 April 1940)

Be sure that the ins and outs of your individuality are no

mystery to Him; and one day they will no longer be a mystery to you. The mould in which a key is made would be a strange thing, if you had never seen a key: and the key itself a strange thing if you had never seen a lock. Your soul has a curious shape because it is a hollow made to fit a particular swelling in the infinite contours of the divine substance, or a key to unlock one of the doors in the house with many mansions. For it is not humanity in the abstract that is to be saved, but you—you, the individual reader, John Stubbs or Janet Smith. Blessed and fortunate creature, your eyes shall behold Him and not another's. . . . Your place in heaven will seem to be made for you and you alone, because you were made for it—made for it stitch by stitch as a glove is made for a hand.

The Problem of Pain, ch. 10

It is a profound mistake to imagine that Christianity ever intended to dissipate the bewilderment and even the terror, the sense of our own nothingness, which come upon us when we think about the nature of things. It comes to intensify them. Without such sensations there is no religion. Many a man, brought up in the glib profession of some shallow form of Christianity, who comes through reading Astronomy to realise for the first time how majestically indifferent most reality is to man, and who perhaps abandons his religion on that account, may at that moment be having his first genuinely religious experience.

Miracles, ch. 7

If Christianity was something we were making up, of course we could make it easier. But it is not. We cannot compete, in simplicity, with people who are inventing religions. How could we? We are dealing with Fact. Of course anyone can be simple if he has no facts to bother about.

Mere Christianity, bk 4, ch. 2

In a sense the converted Jew is the only normal human being in the world. . . . He calls Abraham his father by hereditary right as well as by divine courtesy. He has taken the whole syllabus in order, as it was set; eaten the dinner according to the menu. . . . We ourselves, we christened gentiles, are after all the graft, the wild vine, possessing 'joys not promised to our birth'.

Foreword to Joy Davidman's *Smoke on the Mountain*

When all is said (and truly said) about the divisions of Christendom, there remains, by God's mercy, an enormous common ground.

Preface to *Christian Reflections*

The divisions of Christendom are undeniable. . . . But if any man is tempted to think—as one might be tempted who read only contemporaries—that 'Christianity' is a word of so many meanings that it means nothing at all, he can learn beyond all doubt, by stepping out of his own century, that this is not so. Measured against the ages 'mere Christianity' turns out to be no insipid interdenominational transparency, but something positive, self-consistent, and inexhaustible. . . . We are all rightly distressed, and ashamed also, at the divisions of Christendom. But those who have always lived within the Christian fold may be too easily dispirited by them.

Introduction to *The Incarnation of the Word of God*,
by St Athanasius

When Catholicism goes bad it becomes the world-old, world-wide *religio* of amulets and holy places and priestcraft: Protestantism, in its corresponding decay, becomes a vague mist of ethical platitudes. Catholicism is accused of being much too like all the other religions; Protestantism of being insufficiently like a religion at all. Hence Plato, with his transcendent Forms, is the doctor of Protestants; Aristotle, with his immanent Forms, the doctor of Catholics.

The Allegory of Love, ch. 7, sec. 3

By nature I demand from the arrangements of this world just that permanence which God has expressly refused to give them. . . . I would like everything to be immemorial—to have the same old horizons, the same garden, the same smells and sounds, always there, changeless. The old wine is to me always better. That is, I desire the 'abiding city' where I well know it is not and ought not to be found. . . . We must 'sit light' not only to life itself but to all its phases.

Letters (21 November 1962)

3. SALVATION

'Die before you die. There is no chance after.'

Till We Have Faces, bk 2, ch. 2

Where, except in the present, can the Eternal be met?

'Historicism', *Christian Reflections*

The salvation of a single soul is more important than the production or preservation of all the epics and tragedies in the world.

'Christianity and Literature', *Ibid.*

The glory of God, and, as our only means to glorifying Him, the salvation of human souls, is the real business of life.

'Christianity and Culture', *Ibid.*

In reality, the difference between Biological life and spiritual life is so important that I am going to give them two distinct names. The Biological sort which comes to us through Nature, and which (like everything else in Nature) is always tending to run down and decay so that it can only be kept up by incessant subsidies from Nature in the form of air, water, food, etc., is *Bios*. The Spiritual life which is in God from all eternity, and which made the whole natural universe, is *Zoe*. *Bios* has, to be sure, a certain shadowy or symbolic resemblance to *Zoe*: but only the sort of resemblance there is between a photo and a place, or a statue and a man. A man who changed from having *Bios* to having *Zoe* would have gone through as big a change as a statue which changed from being a carved stone to being a real man.

And that is precisely what Christianity is about. This world is a great sculptor's shop. We are the statues and there is a rumour going round the shop that some of us are some day going to come to life.

Mere Christianity, bk 4, ch. 1

The whole dance, or drama, or pattern of this three-Personal life is to be played out in each one of us: or (putting it the other way round) each one of us has got to enter that pattern, take his place in that dance. There is no other way to the happiness for which we were made. Good things as well as bad, you know, are caught by a kind of infection. If you want to get warm you must stand near the fire: if you want to be wet you must get into the water. If you want joy, power, peace, eternal life, you must get close to, or even into, the thing that has them. They are not a sort of prize which God could, if He chose, just hand out to anyone. They are a great fountain of energy and beauty spurting up at the very centre of reality. If you are close to it, the spray will wet you: if you are not, you will remain dry. Once a man is united to God, how could he not live forever? Once a man is separated from God, what can he do but wither and die?

Ibid., bk 4, ch. 4

It is not enough to want to get rid of one's sins. We also need to believe in the One who saves us from our sins. . . . Because we know that we are sinners, it does not follow that we are saved.

'I Was Decided Upon',
Decision (September 1963)

'Well, exactly the same thing happened again. And I thought to myself, oh dear, how ever many skins have I got to take off? . . . So I scratched away for the third time and got off a third skin, just like the two others, and stepped out of it. But as soon as I looked at myself in the water I knew it had been no good.

'Then the lion said, You will have to let me undress you. . . .

'The very first tear he made was so deep that I thought it had gone right into my heart. And when he began pulling the skin off, it hurt worse than anything I've ever felt. . . . And there it was lying on the grass: only ever so much thicker and darker, and more knobbly looking than the others had been. . . .

'After a bit the lion took me out and dressed me . . . in new clothes—the same I've got on now, as a matter of fact.'

The Voyage of the 'Dawn Treader', ch. 7

I believe that if a million chances were likely to do good, they would be given.

The Problem of Pain, ch. 8

'I hardly know, Sir. What some people say on earth is that the final loss of one soul gives the lie to all the joy of those who are saved.'

'Ye see it does not.'

'I feel in a way that it ought to.'

'That sounds very merciful: but see what lurks behind it.'

'What?'

'The demand of the loveless and the self-imprisoned that they should be allowed to blackmail the universe: that till they consent to be happy (on their own terms) no one else shall taste joy: that theirs should be the final power; that Hell should be able to *veto* Heaven.'

The Great Divorce, ch. 13

If people like you and me find much that we don't naturally like in the public and corporate side of Christianity all the better for us; it will teach us humility and charity towards simple low-brow people who may be better Christians than ourselves. I naturally *loathe* nearly all hymns; the face and life of the charwoman in the next pew who revels in them, teach me that good taste in poetry or music are *not* necessary to salvation.

Letters (7 December 1950)

The puritans were so called because they claimed to be purists or purifiers in ecclesiastical polity: not because they laid more emphasis than other Christians on 'purity' in the sense of chastity. . . . We want, above all, to know what it felt like to be an early Protestant. . . . The experience is that of catastrophic conversion. The man who has passed through it feels like one who has waked from nightmare into ecstasy. Like an accepted lover, he feels that he has done nothing, and never could have done anything to deserve such astonishing happiness. Never again can he 'crow from the dunghill of desert'. All the initiative has been on God's side; all has been free, unbounded grace. And all will continue to be free, unbounded grace. His own puny and ridiculous efforts would be as helpless to retain the joy as they would have been to achieve it in the first place. Fortunately they need not. Bliss is not for sale, cannot be earned. 'Works' have no 'merit', though of course faith, inevitably, even unconsciously, flows out into works of love at once. He is not saved because he does works of love: he does works of love because he is saved. It is faith alone that has saved him: faith bestowed by sheer gift. From this buoyant humility, this farewell to the self with all its good resolutions, anxiety, scruples, and motive-scratchings, all Protestant doctrines originally sprang.

Introduction to *English Literature in the Sixteenth Century*

But it is, I think, a gross exaggeration to picture the saving of a soul as being, normally, at all like the development from seed to flower. The very words repentance, regeneration, the New Man, suggest something very different.

Transposition and Other Addresses, ch. 3

You must picture me alone in that room in Magdalen, night after night, feeling, whenever my mind lifted even for a second from my work, the steady, unrelenting approach of Him whom I so earnestly desired not to meet. That which I greatly feared had at last come upon me. In the Trinity Term of 1929 I gave in, and admitted that God was God, and knelt and prayed: perhaps, that night, the most dejected and reluctant convert in all England. I did not then see what is now the most shining and obvious thing; the Divine humility which will accept a convert even on such terms. . . . The hardness of God is kinder than the softness of men, and His compulsion is our liberation.

Surprised by Joy, ch. 14

'I have come to give myself up,' he said.

'It is well,' said Mother Kirk. 'You have come a long way round to reach this place, whither I would have carried you in a few moments. But it is very well.'

'What must I do?' said John.

'You must take off your rags,' said she, 'as your friend has done already, and then you must dive into this water.'

'Alas,' said he, 'I have never learned to dive.'

'There is nothing to learn,' she said. 'The art of diving is not to do anything new but simply to cease doing something. You have only to let yourself go.'

The Pilgrim's Regress, bk 9, ch. 4

It would, no doubt, have been possible for God to remove by miracle the results of the first sin ever committed by a human being; but this would not have been much good unless He was prepared to remove the results of the second sin, and of the third, and so on forever.

The Problem of Pain, ch. 5

We find thus by experience that there is no good applying to Heaven for earthly comfort. Heaven can give heavenly comfort; no other kind. And earth cannot give earthly comfort either. There is no earthly comfort in the long run.

The Four Loves, ch. 6

4. PRACTISING THE CHRISTIAN LIFE

You never know how much you really believe anything until its truth or falsehood becomes a matter of life and death to you.

A Grief Observed, ch. 2

Do not be scared by the word authority. Believing things on authority only means believing them because you have been told them by someone you think trustworthy. Ninety-nine per cent of the things you believe are believed on authority. I believe there is such a place as New York. I have not seen it myself. I could not prove by abstract reasoning that there must be such a place, I believe it because reliable people have told me so. The ordinary man believes in the Solar System, atoms, evolution, and the circulation of the blood on authority— because the scientists say so. Every historical statement in the world is believed on authority. None of us has seen the Norman Conquest or the defeat of the Armada. None of us could prove them by pure logic as you prove a thing in mathematics. We believe them simply because people who did see them have left writings that tell us about them: in fact, on authority. A man who jibbed at authority in other things as some people do in religion would have to be content to know nothing all his life.

Mere Christianity, bk 2, ch. 5

The moment one asks oneself 'Do I believe?' all belief seems to go. I think this is because one is trying to turn round and look *at* something which is there to be used and work *from*— trying to take out one's eyes instead of keeping them in the right place and seeing *with* them. I find that it happens about other matters as well as faith. In my experience only very robust pleasures will stand the question, 'Am I really enjoying this?' Or attention—the moment I begin thinking about my attention (to a book or a lecture) I have *ipso facto* ceased attending. St. Paul speaks of 'Faith actualized in Love'. And 'the heart is deceitful'; you know better than I how very unreliable introspection is. I should be much more alarmed about your progress if you wrote claiming to be overflowing with Faith, Hope and Charity.

Letters (27 September 1949)

When Christians say the Christ-life is in them, they do not mean simply something mental or moral. When they speak of being 'in Christ' or of Christ being 'in them', this is not simply a way of saying that they are thinking about Christ or copying Him. They mean that Christ is actually operating through them; that the whole mass of Christians are the

physical organism through which Christ acts—that we are
His fingers and muscles, the cells of His body.

Mere Christianity, bk 2, ch. 5

How little people know who think that holiness is dull.
When one meets the real thing . . . it is irresistible. If even ten
per cent of the world's population had it, would not the whole
world be converted and happy before a year's end?

Unpublished letter (1 August 1953)

There must perhaps always be just enough lack of demonstrative certainty to make free choice possible; for what could
we do but accept if the faith were like the multiplication table?

Encounter with Light

When you are asked for trust you may give it or withhold it; it is senseless to say that you will trust if you are given
demonstrative certainty. There would be no room for trust if
demonstration were given.

The World's Last Night, ch. 2

If we wish to be rational, not now and then, but constantly,
we must pray for the gift of Faith, for the power to go on
believing, not in the teeth of reason, but in the teeth of lust, and
terror, and jealousy, and boredom, and indifference, that which
reason, authority, or experience, or all three, have once de-
livered to us for truth.

'Religion: Reality or Substitute?'
Christian Reflections

Faith may mean (a) A settled intellectual assent. In that sense
faith (or 'belief') in God hardly differs from faith in the uniformity of Nature or in the consciousness of other people.
This is what, I think, has sometimes been called a 'notional' or

'intellectual' or 'carnal' faith. It may also mean (b) A trust, or confidence, in the God whose existence is thus assented to. This involves an attitude of the will. It is more like our confidence in a friend. It would be generally agreed that Faith in sense A is not a religious state. The devils who 'believe and tremble' have Faith A. A man who curses or ignores God may have Faith A. Philosophical arguments for the existence of God are presumably intended to produce Faith A because it is a necessary pre-condition of Faith B, and in that sense their ultimate intention is religious. But their immediate object, the conclusion they attempt to prove, is not. I therefore think they cannot be justly accused of trying to get a religious conclusion out of non-religious premises. I agree . . . that this cannot be done; but I deny that the religious philosophers are trying to do it.

'Is Theism Important? A Reply',
Socratic Digest (1952)

We must admit that Faith, as we know it, does not flow from philosophical argument alone; nor from experience of the Numinous alone; nor from moral experience alone; nor from history alone; but from historical events which at once will fulfil and transcend the moral category, which link themselves with the most numinous elements in Paganism, and which (as it seems to us) demand as their pre-supposition the existence of a Being who is more, but not less, than the God whom many reputable philosophers think they can establish.

Ibid.

Do not be deceived, Wormwood. Our cause is never more in danger than when a human, no longer desiring, but still intending, to do our Enemy's will, looks round upon a universe from which every trace of Him seems to have vanished, and asks why he has been forsaken, and still obeys.

The Screwtape Letters, ch. 8

If you examined a hundred people who had lost their faith in Christianity, I wonder how many of them would turn out to have been reasoned out of it by honest argument? Do not most people simply drift away?

Mere Christianity, bk 3, ch. 11

The very man who has argued you down will sometimes be found, years later, to have been influenced by what you said.

Reflections on the Psalms, ch. 7

'There have been men before now who got so interested in proving the existence of God that they came to care nothing for God Himself . . . as if the good Lord had nothing to do but *exist*! There have been some who were so occupied in spreading Christianity that they never gave a thought to Christ.'

The Great Divorce, ch. 9

A man who really believes that 'Heaven' is in the sky may well, in his heart, have a far truer and more spiritual conception of it than many a modern logician who could expose that fallacy with a few strokes of his pen.

Miracles, ch. 16

Just as the Christian has his moments when the clamour of this visible and audible world is so persistent and the whisper of the spiritual world so faint that faith and reason can hardly stick to their guns, so, as I well remember, the atheist too has his moments of shuddering misgiving, of an all but irresistible suspicion that old tales may after all be true, that something or someone from outside may at any moment break into his neat, explicable, mechanical universe. Believe in God and you will have to face hours when it seems *obvious* that this material world is the only reality: disbelieve in Him and you must face hours when this material world seems to shout at you that it is *not* all. No conviction, religious or irreligious, will, of itself, end once and for all this fifth-columnist in the soul. Only the practice of Faith resulting in the habit of Faith will gradually do that.

'Religion: Reality or Substitute?'
Christian Reflections

'Why is it called Aslan's table?' asked Lucy presently.
'It is set here by his bidding. . . .'
'But how does the food *keep*?' asked the practical Eustace.
'It is eaten, and renewed, every day,' said the girl.

The Voyage of the 'Dawn Treader', ch. 13

'Give us our daily bread' (not an annuity for life) applies to spiritual gifts too; the little *daily* support for the *daily* trial. Life has to be taken day by day and hour by hour.

Letters (17 July 1953)

Relying on God has to begin all over again every day as if nothing had yet been done.

Ibid. (*c.* September 1949)

Thank God he has not allowed my *faith* to be greatly tempted by the present horrors. I do not doubt that whatever misery He permits will be for our ultimate good unless by rebellious will we convert it to evil. But I get no further than Gethsemane: and am daily thankful that that scene of all others in Our Lord's life did not go unrecorded. . . . The process of living seems to consist in coming to realize truths so ancient and simple that, if stated, they sound like barren platitudes.

Ibid. (8 May 1939)

If you ask why we should obey God, in the last resort the answer is, 'I am.' To know God is to know that our obedience is due to Him.

Surprised by Joy, ch. 15

Obedience is the road to freedom, humility the road to pleasure, unity the road to personality.

Transposition and Other Addresses, ch. 3

Nor must we postpone obedience to a precept until its credentials have been examined. Only those who are practising the *Tao* will understand it. It is the well-nurtured man, the *cuor gentil*, and he alone, who can recognize Reason when it comes. It is Paul, the Pharisee, the man 'perfect as touching the Law' who learns where and how that Law was deficient.

The Abolition of Man, ch. 2

'Where can you taste the joy of obeying unless He bids you do something for which His bidding is the *only* reason?'

Perelandra, ch. 9

'All His biddings are joys.'

Ibid., ch. 6

For however important chastity (or courage, or truthfulness, or any other virtue) may be, this process [trying again after failure] trains us in habits of the soul which are more important still. It cures our illusions about ourselves and teaches us to depend on God. We learn, on the one hand, that we cannot trust ourselves even in our best moments, and, on the other, that we need not despair even in our worst, for our failures are forgiven. The only fatal thing is to sit down content with anything less than perfection.

Mere Christianity, bk 3, ch. 5

Obedience is the key to all doors; *feelings* come (or don't come) and go as God pleases.

Letters (7 December 1950)

We might think that God wanted simply obedience to a set of rules: whereas He really wants people of a particular sort.

Mere Christianity, bk 3, ch. 2

Nothing gives one a more spuriously good conscience than keeping rules, even if there has been a total absence of all real charity and faith.

Unpublished letter (20 February 1955)

Because we love something else more than this world we love even this world better than those who know no other.

'Some Thoughts', *The First Decade*

Perhaps, for many of us, all experience merely defines, so to speak, the shape of that gap where our love of God ought to be. It is not enough. It is something. If we cannot 'practice the presence of God', it is something to practice the absence of God, to become increasingly aware of our unawareness till we feel like men who should stand beside a great cataract and hear no noise, or like a man in a story who looks in a mirror and finds no face there, or a man in a dream who stretches out his hand to visible objects and gets no sensation of touch. To know that one is dreaming is to be no longer perfectly asleep.

The Four Loves, ch. 6

Every Christian would agree that a man's spiritual health is exactly proportional to his love for God.

Ibid., ch. 1

The allegorical sense of [St Mary Magdalene's] great action dawned on me the other day. The precious alabaster box which one must *break* over the Holy Feet is one's *heart*. Easier said than done. And the contents become perfume only when it is broken. While they are safe inside they are more like sewage.

Unpublished letter (1 November 1954)

A Christian society is not going to arrive until most of us really want it: and we are not going to want it until we become fully Christian. I may repeat 'Do as you would be done by' till I am black in the face, but I cannot really carry it out till I love my neighbour as myself: and I cannot learn to love my neighbour as myself till I learn to love God: and I cannot learn to love God except by learning to obey Him. And so . . . we are driven on to something more inward—driven on from social matters to religious matters.

Mere Christianity, bk 3, ch. 3

When I have learnt to love God better than my earthly dearest, I shall love my earthly dearest better than I do now. In so far as I learn to love my earthly dearest at the expense of God and *instead* of God, I shall be moving towards the state in which I shall not love my earthly dearest at all. When first things are put first, second things are not suppressed but increased.

Letters (8 November 1952)

I would prefer to combat the 'I'm special' feeling not by the thought 'I'm no more special than anyone else', but by the feeling 'Everyone is as special as me'. In one way there is no difference, I grant, for both remove the specialty. But there is a difference in another way. The first might lead you to think, 'I'm only one of the crowd like everyone else'. But the second leads to the truth that there isn't any crowd. No one is like anyone else. All are 'members' (organs) in the Body of Christ. All different and all necessary to the whole and to one another; each loved by God individually, as if it were the only creature in existence. Otherwise you might get the idea that God is like the government which can only deal with the people in the mass.

Ibid. (20 June 1952)

A *perfect* man would never act from sense of duty; he'd always *want* the right thing more than the wrong one. Duty is only a substitute for love (of God and of other people) like a crutch which is a substitute for a leg. Most of us need the crutch at times; but of course it is idiotic to use the crutch when our own legs (our own loves, tastes, habits etc.) can do the journey on their own.

Ibid. (18 July 1957)

Do not waste time bothering whether you 'love' your neighbour; act as if you did. As soon as we do this we find one of the great secrets. When you are behaving as if you loved someone, you will presently come to love him. If you injure someone you dislike, you will find yourself disliking him more. If you do him a good turn, you will find yourself disliking him less.

Mere Christianity, bk 3, ch. 9

We ought perhaps to regard the work of miracles, however rare, as the true Christian norm and ourselves as spiritual cripples.

'Petitionary Prayer', *Christian Reflections*

We might try to understand exactly what loving your neighbour as yourself means. I have to love him as I love myself. Well, how exactly do I love myself?

Now that I come to think of it, I have not exactly got a feeling of fondness or affection for myself, and I do not even always enjoy my own society. So apparently 'Love your neighbour' does not mean 'feel fond of him' or 'find him attractive'. I ought to have seen that before, because, of course, you cannot feel fond of a person by trying. Do I think well of myself, think myself a nice chap? Well, I am afraid I sometimes do (and those are, no doubt, my worst moments) but that is not why I love myself. In fact it is the other way round: my self-love makes me think myself nice, but thinking myself nice is not why I love myself. So loving my enemies does not apparently mean thinking them nice either.

Mere Christianity, bk 3, ch. 7

The love we are commanded to have for God and our neighbour is a state of the *will*, not of the affections (though if they ever also play their part so much the better).

Letters (c. March 1956)

I am thinking of Mrs. Fidget, who died a few months ago. It is really astonishing how her family have brightened up. The drawn look has gone from her husband's face; he begins to be able to laugh. The younger boy, whom I had always thought an embittered, peevish little creature, turns out to be quite human. The elder, who was hardly ever at home except when he was in bed, is nearly always there now and has begun to re-organise the garden. The girl, who was always supposed to be 'delicate' (though I never found out what exactly the trouble was), now has the riding lessons which were once out of the question, dances all night, and plays any amount of tennis. Even the dog who was never allowed out except on a lead is now a well-known member of the Lamp-post Club in their road.

Mrs. Fidget very often said that she lived for her family. And it was not untrue. Everyone in the neighborhood knew it. . . .

The Vicar says Mrs. Fidget is now at rest. Let us hope she is.

The Four Loves, ch. 3

Did we pretend to be angry about one thing when we knew, or could have known, that our anger had a different and much less presentable cause? Did we pretend to be 'hurt' in our sensitive and tender feelings . . . when envy, ungratified vanity, or thwarted self-will was our real trouble? Such tactics often succeed. The other parties give in. They give in not because they don't know what is really wrong with us but because they have long known it only too well. . . . It needs surgery which they know we will never face. And so we win; by cheating. But the unfairness is very deeply felt. Indeed what is commonly called 'sensitiveness' is the most powerful engine of domestic tyranny, sometimes a lifelong tyranny.

Reflections on the Psalms, ch. 2

Did I hate him, then? Indeed, I believe so. A love like that can grow to be nine-tenths hatred and still call itself love.

Till We Have Faces, bk 2, ch. 1

Fallen man is not simply an imperfect creature who needs improvement: he is a rebel who must lay down his arms. . . . This process of surrender—this movement full speed astern— is what Christians call repentance. Now repentance is no fun at all. It is something much harder than merely eating humble pie. It means unlearning all the self-conceit and self-will that we have been training ourselves into for thousands of years. It means killing part of yourself, undergoing a kind of death. In fact, it needs a good man to repent. And here comes the catch. Only a bad person needs to repent: only a good person can repent perfectly. The worse you are the more you need it and the less you can do it. The only person who could do it perfectly would be a perfect person—and he would not need it.

Mere Christianity, bk 2, ch. 4

We need to forgive our brother seventy times seven not only for 490 offences but for one offence.

Reflections on the Psalms, ch. 3

It is always just possible that Jesus Christ meant what He said when He told us to seek the secret place and to close the door.

'Heaven, Earth and Outer Space',
Decision (October 1963)

Prayer is either a sheer illusion or a personal contact between embryonic, incomplete persons (ourselves) and the utterly concrete Person. Prayer in the sense of petition, asking for things, is a small part of it; confession and penitence are its threshold, adoration its sanctuary, the presence and vision and enjoyment of God its bread and wine. In it God shows Himself to us.

The World's Last Night, ch. 1

Now the disquieting thing is not simply that we skimp and begrudge the duty of prayer. The really disquieting thing is it should have to be numbered among duties at all. For we believe that we were created 'to glorify God and enjoy Him forever'. And if the few, the very few, minutes we now spend on intercourse with God are a burden to us rather than a delight, what then? If I were a Calvinist this symptom would fill me with despair. What can be done *for*—or what should be done *with*—a rose-tree that *dislikes* producing roses? Surely it ought to want to? . . .

If we were perfected, prayer would not be a duty, it would be delight. Some day, please God, it will be. The same is true of many other behaviours which now appear as duties. If I loved my neighbour as myself, most of the actions which are now my moral duty would flow out of me as spontaneously as song from a lark or fragrance from a flower. Why is this not so yet? . . . The very activities for which we were created are, while we live on earth, variously impeded: by evil in ourselves or in others. Not to practise them is to abandon our humanity. To practise them spontaneously and delightfully is not yet possible. This situation creates the category of duty, the whole specifically *moral* realm. . . .

I must say my prayers to-day whether I feel devout or not; but that is only as I must learn my grammar if I am ever to read the poets.

Letters to Malcolm, ch. 21

The advantage of a fixed form of service is that we know what is coming. *Ex tempore* public prayer has this difficulty; we don't know whether we can mentally join in it until we've heard it—it might be phoney or heretical. We are therefore called upon to carry on a *critical* and a *devotional* activity at the same moment: two things hardly compatible. In a fixed form we ought to have 'gone through the motions' before in our private prayers; the rigid form really sets our devotions *free*. I also find the more rigid it is, the easier it is to keep one's thoughts from straying. Also it prevents getting too completely eaten up by whatever happens to be the preoccupation of the moment (i.e. war, an election, or what not). The *permanent* shape of Christianity shows through. I don't see how the *ex tempore* method can help becoming provincial, and I think it has a great tendency to direct attention to the minister rather than to God.

Letters (1 April 1952)

The efficacy of prayer is . . . no *more* of a problem than the efficacy of *all* human acts, i.e., if you say 'It is useless to pray because Providence already knows what is best and will certainly do it', then why is it not equally useless (and for the same reason) to try to alter the course of events in any way whatever?

Ibid. (21 February 1932)

If there is—as the very concept of prayer presupposes—an adaptation between the free actions of men in prayer and the course of events, this adaptation is from the beginning inherent in the great single creative act. Our prayers are heard—don't say 'have been heard' or you are putting God into time—not only before we make them but before we are made ourselves.

Letters to Malcolm, ch. 9

That wisdom must sometimes refuse what ignorance may quite innocently ask seems to be self-evident.

'Petitionary Prayer', *Christian Reflections*

> . . . if His action lingers
> Till men have prayed, and suffers their weak prayers indeed
> To move as very muscles His delaying fingers,
> Who, in His longanimity and love for our
> Small dignities, enfeebles, for a time, His power.
>
> 'Sonnet', *Poems*

Provided that meetings, pamphlets, policies, movements, causes, and crusade, matter more to him than prayers and sacraments and charity, he is ours—and the more 'religious' (on those terms) the more securely ours. I could show you a pretty cageful down here.

The Screwtape Letters, ch. 7

[Our Vicar] assures me that, so far as he has been able to discover, the overwhelming majority of his parishioners mean by 'saying their prayers' repeating whatever little formula they were taught in childhood by their mothers. I wonder how this can come about. It can't be that they are never penitent or thankful—they're dear people, many of them—or have no needs. Is it that there is a sort of water-tight bulk-head between their 'religion' and their 'real life', in which case the part of their life which they call 'religious' is really the irreligious part?

Letters to Malcolm, ch. 12

A sin once repented and forgiven, is gone, annihilated, burnt up in the fire of Divine Love, white as snow. There is no harm in continuing to 'bewail' it, i.e. to express one's sorrow, but not to ask for pardon, for that you have already—one's sorrow for being that sort of person.

Letters (8 January 1952)

We must beware of the past, mustn't we? I mean that any fixing of the mind on old evils beyond what is absolutely necessary for repenting our own sins and forgiving those of others is certainly useless and usually bad for us.

Unpublished letter (5 June 1961)

I think that if God forgives us we must forgive ourselves. Otherwise it is almost like setting up ourselves as a higher tribunal than Him.

Letters (9 April 1951)

[In Confession] there is the gain in self-knowledge; most of us have never really faced the facts about ourselves until we uttered them aloud in plain words, calling a spade a spade.

Ibid. (6-7 April 1953)

It is no use to ask God with factitious earnestness for A when our whole mind is in reality filled with the desire for B. We must lay before Him what is in us, not what ought to be in us.

Letters to Malcolm, ch. 4

'Don't you remember on earth—there were things too hot to touch with your finger but you could drink them all right? Shame is like that. If you will accept it—if you will drink the cup to the bottom—you will find it very nourishing: but try to do anything else with it and it scalds.'

The Great Divorce, ch. 7

It also seemed to me that forgiving (that man's cruelty) and being forgiven (my resentment) were the very same thing. 'Forgive and you shall be forgiven' sounds like a bargain. But perhaps it is something much more. By heavenly standards, that is, for pure intelligence, it is perhaps a tautology—forgiving and being forgiven are two names for the same thing. The important thing is that a discord has been resolved, and it is certainly the great Resolver who has done it.

Letters to Malcolm, ch. 20

In solitude, and also in confession, I have found (to my regret) that the degrees of shame and disgust which I actually feel at my own sins do not at all correspond to what my reason tells me about their comparative gravity. Just as the degree to which, in daily life, I feel the emotion of fear has very little to do with my rational judgement of the danger. . . . I have confessed ghastly uncharities with less reluctance than small unmentionables—or those sins which happen to be ungentlemanly as well as un-Christian. Our emotional reactions to our own behaviour are of limited ethical significance.

Ibid., ch. 18

If we cannot lay down our [temperamental] tastes along with our other carnal baggage, at the church door, surely we should at least bring them in to be humbled and, if necessary, modified, not to be indulged.

Letter in *Church Times* (10 August 1951)

One cannot establish the efficacy of prayer by statistics. . . . It remains a matter of faith and of God's personal action; it could become a matter of demonstration only if it were impersonal or mechanical. When I say 'personal' I do not mean private or individual. All our prayers are united with Christ's perpetual prayer and are part of the Church's prayer.

Letters (*c*. January 1951)

When you pray for Hitler and Stalin how do you actually teach yourself to make the prayer real? The two things that help me are (*a*) A continual grasp of the idea that one is only joining one's feeble little voice to the perpetual intercession of Christ who died for these very men. (*b*) A recollection, as firm as I can make it, of all one's own cruelty; which might have blossomed under different conditions into something terrible. You and I are not at bottom so different from these ghastly creatures.

Ibid. (16 April 1940)

The prayer preceding all prayers is 'May it be the real I who speaks. May it be the real Thou that I speak to.' Infinitely various are the levels from which we pray. Emotional intensity is in itself no proof of spiritual depth. If we pray in terror we shall pray earnestly; it only proves that terror is an earnest emotion. Only God Himself can let the bucket down to the depths in us. And, on the other side, He must constantly work as the iconoclast. Every idea of Him we form, He must in mercy shatter. The most blessed result of prayer would be to rise thinking 'But I never knew before. I never dreamed . . .' I suppose it was at such a moment that Thomas Aquinas said of all his own theology, 'It reminds me of straw.'

Letters to Malcolm, ch. 15

Like everyone else I had been told as a child that one must not only say one's prayers but think about what one was saying. Accordingly, when I came to a serious belief, I tried to put this into practice. At first it seemed plain sailing. But soon the false conscience . . . came into play. One had no sooner reached 'Amen' than it whispered, 'Yes. But are you sure you were really thinking about what you said?' . . .

I set myself a standard. No clause of my prayer was to be allowed to pass muster unless it was accompanied by what I called a 'realisation', by which I meant a certain vividness of the imagination and the affections. . . . If only someone had read to me old Walter Hilton's warning that we must never in prayer strive to extort 'by maistry' what God does not give! But no one did; and night after night, dizzy with desire for sleep and often in a kind of despair, I endeavoured to pump up my 'realisations'. . . . Had I pursued the same road much further I think I should have gone mad.

Surprised by Joy, ch. 4

There are, no doubt, passages in the New Testament which may seem at first sight to promise an invariable granting of our prayers. But that cannot be what they really mean. For in the very heart of the story we meet a glaring instance to the contrary. In Gethsemane the holiest of all petitioners prayed three times that a certain cup might pass from Him. It did not. After that the idea that prayer is recommended to us as a sort of infallible gimmick may be dismissed. . . .

Invariable 'success' in prayer would not prove the Christian doctrine at all. It would prove something much more like magic—a power in certain human beings to control, or compel, the course of nature.

The World's Last Night, ch. 1

The gnat-like cloud of petty anxieties and decisions about the conduct of the next hour have interfered with my prayers more often than any passion or appetite whatever.

The Four Loves, ch. 5

It's so much easier to pray . . . than go and see him.

Letters to Malcolm, ch. 12

Can we believe that God ever really modifies His action in response to the suggestions of men? For infinite wisdom does not need telling what is best, and infinite goodness needs no urging to do it. But neither does God need any of those things that are done by finite agents, whether living or inanimate. He could, if He chose, repair our bodies miraculously without food; or give us food without the aid of farmers, bakers and butchers; or knowledge without the aid of learned men; or convert the heathen without missionaries. Instead, He allows soils and weather and animals and the muscles, minds, and wills of men to co-operate in the execution of His Will. 'God,' said Pascal, 'instituted prayer in order to lend to His creatures the dignity of causality.' . . .

He seems to do nothing of Himself which He can possibly delegate to His creatures.

The World's Last Night, ch. 1

Don't forget to use the 'heads I win, tails you lose' argument. If the thing he prays for doesn't happen, then that is one more proof that petitionary prayers don't work; if it does happen, he will, of course, be able to see some of the physical causes which led up to it, and 'therefore it would have happened anyway', and thus a granted prayer becomes just as good a proof as a denied one that prayers are ineffective.

The Screwtape Letters, ch. 27

A man who knew empirically that an event had been caused by his prayer would feel like a magician. His head would turn and his heart would be corrupted. The Christian is not to ask whether this or that event happened because of a prayer. He is rather to believe that all events without exception are *answers* to prayer in the sense that whether they are grantings or refusals the prayers of all concerned and their needs have all been taken into account. All prayers are heard, though not all prayers are granted. We must not picture destiny as a film unrolling for the most part on its own, but in which our prayers are sometimes allowed to insert additional items. On the contrary; what the film displays to us as it unrolls already contains the results of our prayers and of all our other acts.

Miracles, Appendix B

The worse one is praying, the longer one's prayers take. . . .
I have a notion that what seem our worst prayers may really be, in God's eyes, our best. Those, I mean, which are least supported by devotional feeling and contend with the greatest disinclination. For these, perhaps, being nearly all will, come from a deeper level than feeling. In feeling there is so much that is really not ours—so much that comes from weather and health or from the last book read. One thing seems certain. It is no good angling for the rich moments. God sometimes seems to speak to us most intimately when He catches us, as it were, off our guard. Our preparations to receive Him sometimes have

the opposite effect. Doesn't Charles Williams say somewhere that 'the altar must often be built in one place in order that the fire from heaven may descend *somewhere else*'?

Letters to Malcolm, ch. 21

Perhaps, as those who do not turn to God in petty trials will have no *habit* or such resort to help them when the great trials come, so those who have not learned to ask Him for childish things will have less readiness to ask Him for great ones. We must not be too high-minded. I fancy we may sometimes be deterred from small prayers by a sense of our own dignity rather than of God's.

Ibid., ch. 4

I mentioned to a distinguished theologian that I had been attacked by 'a man called N.', and he replied 'Oh! old P. N.! What does he believe *this week*?'—so apparently he changes his views fairly often. Perhaps one day he may give Christianity a trial. I have put him in my prayers.

Unpublished letter (26 January 1959)

When I first began to draw near to belief in God and even for some time after it had been given to me, I found a stumbling block in the demand so clamorously made by all religious people that we should 'praise' God; still more in the suggestion that God Himself demanded it. . . . What do we mean when we say that a picture is 'admirable'? . . . The sense in which the picture 'deserves' or 'demands' admiration is rather this, that admiration is the correct, adequate or appropriate, response to it, that, if paid, admiration will not be 'thrown away', and that if we do not admire we shall be stupid, insensible, and great losers, we shall have missed something. . . . He is that Object to admire which (or, if you like, to appreciate which) is simply to be awake, to have entered the real world; not to appreciate which is to have lost the greatest experience, and in the end to have lost all. . . .

I did not see that it is in the process of being worshipped that God communicates His presence to men.

Reflections on the Psalms, ch. 9

I had never noticed that all enjoyment spontaneously overflows into praise unless (sometimes even if) shyness or the fear of boring others is deliberately brought in to check it. . . . I had not noticed how the humblest, and at the same time most balanced and capacious, minds, praised most, while the cranks, misfits and malcontents praised least. The good critics found something to praise in many imperfect works; the bad ones continually narrowed the list of books we might be allowed to read. The healthy and unaffected man, even if luxuriously brought up and widely experienced in good cookery, could praise a very modest meal: the dyspeptic and the snob found fault with all. Except where intolerably adverse circumstances interfere, praise almost seems to be inner health made audible. . . . I had not noticed either that just as men spontaneously praise whatever they value, so they spontaneously urge us to join them in praising it: 'Isn't she lovely? Wasn't it glorious? Don't you think that magnificent?' The Psalmists in telling everyone to praise God are doing what all men do when they speak of what they care about.

Ibid.

I think we delight to praise what we enjoy because the praise not merely expresses but completes the enjoyment; it is its appointed consummation. It is not out of compliment that lovers keep on telling one another how beautiful they are; the delight is incomplete till it is expressed. . . . If it were possible for a created soul fully (I mean, up to the full measure conceivable in a finite being) to 'appreciate', that is to love and delight in, the worthiest object of all, and simultaneously at every moment to give this delight perfect expression, then that soul would be in supreme beatitude. It is along these lines that I find it easiest to understand the Christian doctrine that 'Heaven' is a state in which angels now, and men hereafter, are perpetually employed in praising God. . . . To see what the doctrine really means, we must suppose ourselves to be in perfect love with God—drunk with, drowned in, dissolved by, that delight which, far from remaining pent up within ourselves as incommunicable, hence hardly tolerable, bliss, flows out from us incessantly again in effortless and perfect expression, our joy no more separable from the praise in which it liberates and utters itself than the brightness a mirror receives is separable from the brightness it sheds.

Ibid.

Gratitude exclaims, very properly, 'How good of God to give me this.' Adoration says, 'What must be the quality of that Being whose far-off and momentary coruscations are like this!' One's mind runs back up the sunbeam to the sun.

Letters to Malcolm, ch. 17

Most men must glorify God by doing to His glory something which is not *per se* an act of glorifying but which becomes so by being offered. . . . The work of a charwoman and the work of a poet become spiritual in the same way and on the same condition.

'Christianity and Culture',
Christian Reflections

Praise is the mode of love which always has some element of joy in it.

A Grief Observed, ch. 4

When our participation in a rite becomes perfect we think no more of ritual, but are engrossed by that *about which* the rite is performed; but afterwards we recognize that ritual was the sole method by which this concentration could be achieved.

A Preface to 'Paradise Lost', ch. 8

As long as you notice, and have to count the steps, you are not yet dancing but only learning to dance. A good shoe is a shoe you don't notice. Good reading becomes possible when you need not consciously think about eyes, or light, or print, or spelling. The perfect church service would be one we were almost unaware of; our attention would have been on God.

Letters to Malcolm, ch. 1

The society into which the Christian is called at baptism is not a collective but a Body. It is in fact that Body of which the family is an image on the natural level. If anyone came to it with the misconception that membership of the Church was membership in a debased modern sense—a massing together of persons as if they were pennies or counters—he would be corrected at the threshold by the discovery that the Head of this Body is so unlike the inferior members that they share no predicate with Him save by analogy. We are summoned from the outset to combine as creatures with our Creator, as mortals with immortal, as redeemed sinners with sinless Redeemer. His presence, the interaction between Him and us, must always be the overwhelmingly dominant factor in the life we are to lead within the Body: and any conception of Christian fellowship which does not mean primarily fellowship with Him is out of court.

Transposition and Other Addresses, ch. 3

A row of identically dressed and identically trained soldiers set side by side, or a number of citizens listed as voters in a constituency, are not members of anything in the Pauline sense. I am afraid that when we describe a man as 'a member of the Church' we usually mean nothing Pauline: we mean only that he is a unit—that he is one more specimen of the same kind of thing as X and Y and Z. How true membership in a body differs from inclusion in a collective may be seen in the structure of a family. The grandfather, the parents, the grown-up son, the child, the dog, and the cat are true members (in the organic sense) precisely because they are not members or units of a homogeneous class. They are not interchangeable. Each person is almost a species in himself. The mother is not simply a different person from the daughter, she is a different kind of person. The grown-up brother is not simply one unit in the class children, he is a separate estate of the realm. The father and grandfather are almost as different as the cat and the dog. If you subtract any one member you have not simply reduced the family in number, you have inflicted an injury on its structure. Its unity is a unity of unlikes, almost of incommensurables.

Ibid.

I have been told of a very small and very devout boy who was heard murmuring to himself on Easter morning a poem of his own composition which began 'Chocolate eggs and Jesus risen'. This seems to me, for his age, both admirable poetry and admirable piety. But of course the time will soon come when such a child can no longer effortlessly and spontaneously enjoy that unity. He will become able to distinguish the spiritual from the ritual and festal aspect of Easter; chocolate eggs will no longer be sacramental. And once he has distinguished he must put one or the other first. If he puts the spiritual first he can still taste something of Easter in the chocolate eggs; if he puts the eggs first they will soon be no more than any other sweetmeat. They have taken on an independent, and therefore a soon withering, life.

Reflections on the Psalms, ch. 5

Enemy-occupied territory—that is what this world is. Christianity is the story of how the rightful king has landed, you might say landed in disguise, and is calling us all to take part in a great campaign of sabotage. When you go to church you are really listening in to the secret wireless from our friends: that is why the enemy is so anxious to prevent us from going. He does it by playing on our conceit and laziness and intellectual snobbery.

Mere Christianity, bk 2, ch. 2

Man needs to be triply protected by humility if he is to eat the bread of angels without risk.

The Four Loves, ch. 4

It is 'sweet, sweet, sweet poison' to feel able to imply 'thus saith the Lord' at the end of every expression of our pet aversions.

'Christianity and Culture', *Christian Reflections*

The modern habit of doing ceremonial things unceremoniously is no proof of humility; rather it proves the offender's inability to forget himself in the rite, and his readiness to spoil for every one else the proper pleasure of ritual.

A Preface to 'Paradise Lost', ch. 3

You must therefore conceal from the patient the true end of Humility. Let him think of it not as self-forgetfulness but as a certain kind of opinion (namely, a low opinion) of his own talents and character. Some talents, I gather, he really has. Fix in his mind the idea that humility consists in trying to believe those talents to be less valuable than he believes them to be.

The Screwtape Letters, ch. 14

Perfect humility dispenses with modesty.

Transposition and Other Addresses, ch. 2

One is sometimes (not often) glad not to be a great theologian; one might so easily mistake it for being a good Christian.

Reflections on the Psalms, ch. 6

The proper good of a creature is to surrender itself to its Creator—to enact intellectually, volitionally, and emotionally, that relationship which is given in the mere fact of its being a creature. . . . In the world as we now know it, the problem is how to recover this self-surrender. We are not merely imperfect creatures who must be improved: we are, as Newman said, rebels who must lay down our arms. . . . To surrender a self-will inflamed and swollen with years of usurpation is a kind of death. . . . Hence the necessity to die daily: however often we think we have broken the rebellious self we shall still find it alive.

The Problem of Pain, ch. 6

I am, indeed, far from agreeing with those who think all religious fear barbarous and degrading and demand that it should be banished from the spiritual life. Perfect love, we know, casteth out fear. But so do several other things—ignorance, alcohol, passion, presumption, and stupidity. It is very desirable that we should all advance to that perfection of love in which we shall fear no longer; but it is very undesirable, until we have reached that stage, that we should allow any inferior agent to cast out our fear.

The World's Last Night, ch. 7

Though we struggle against things because we are afraid of them, it is often the other way round—we get afraid *because* we struggle.

Unpublished letter (17 June 1963)

I am inclined to think a Christian would be wise to avoid,

where he decently can, any meeting with people who are bullies, lascivious, cruel, dishonest, spiteful and so forth.

Not because we are 'too good' for them. In a sense because we are not good enough. We are not good enough to cope with all the temptations, nor clever enough to cope with all the problems, which an evening spent in such society produces. The temptation is to condone, to connive at; by our words, looks and laughter, to 'consent'.

Reflections on the Psalms, ch. 7

Pray for me; I am suffering incessant temptations to uncharitable thoughts at present; one of those black moods in which nearly all one's friends seem to be selfish or even false. And how terrible that there should be even a kind of *pleasure* in thinking evil.

Letters (12 January 1950)

The real difficulty is . . . to adapt one's steady beliefs about tribulation to this *particular* tribulation: for the particular, when it arrives, always seems so peculiarly intolerable.

Ibid. (2 June 1940)

We must not be Pharisaical even to the Pharisees.

Reflections on the Psalms, ch. 7

One of the marks of a certain type of bad man is that he cannot give up a thing himself without wanting every one else to give it up. That is not the Christian way. An individual Christian may see fit to give up all sorts of things for special reasons—marriage, or meat, or beer, or the cinema; but the moment he starts saying the things are bad in themselves, or looking down his nose at other people who do use them, he has taken the wrong turning.

Mere Christianity, bk 3, ch. 2

It was not for societies or states that Christ died, but for men. In that sense Christianity must seem to secular collectivists to involve an almost frantic assertion of individuality. But then it is not the individual as such who will share Christ's victory over death. We shall share the victory by being in the Victor. A rejection, or in Scripture's strong language, a crucifixion of the natural self is the passport to everlasting life. Nothing that has not died will be resurrected. That is just how Christianity cuts across the antithesis between individualism and collectivism. There lies the maddening ambiguity of our faith as it must appear to outsiders. It sets its face relentlessly against our natural individualism; on the other hand, it gives back to those who abandon individualism an eternal possession of their own personal being, even of their bodies. As mere biological entities, each with its separate will to live and to expand, we are apparently of no account; we are cross-fodder. But as organs in the Body of Christ, as stones and pillars in the temple, we are assured of our eternal self-identity and shall live to remember the galaxies as an old tale.

Transposition and Other Addresses, ch. 3

I know all about the despair of overcoming chronic temptations. It is not serious, provided self-offended petulance, annoyance at breaking records, impatience etc. don't get the upper hand. *No amount* of falls will really undo us if we keep on picking ourselves up each time. We shall of course be very muddy and tattered children by the time we reach home. But the bathrooms are all ready, the towels put out, and the clean clothes in the airing cupboard. The only fatal thing is to lose one's temper and give it up. It is when we notice the dirt that God is most present in us; it is the very sign of His presence.

Letters (20 January 1942)

I suppose the only way with thorns in the flesh (until one can get them out) is not to press on the place where they are embedded.

Unpublished letter (26 June 1955)

Never, in peace or war, commit your virtue or your happiness to the future. Happy work is best done by the man who takes his long-term plans somewhat lightly and works from moment to moment 'as to the Lord'. It is only our *daily* bread that we are encouraged to ask for. The present is the only time in which any duty can be done or any grace received.

Transposition and Other Addresses, ch. 4

It seems to me that we often, almost sulkily, reject the good that God offers us because, at that moment, we expected some other good. . . . On every level of our life—in our religious experience, in our gastronomic, erotic, aesthetic, and social experience—we are always harking back to some occasion which seemed to us to reach perfection, setting that up as·a norm, and depreciating all other occasions by comparison. But these other occasions, I now suspect, are often full of their own new blessing, if only we would lay ourselves open to it. God shows us a new facet of the glory, and we refuse to look at it because we're still looking for the old one. And of course we don't get that. You can't, at the twentieth reading, get again the experience of reading *Lycides* for the first time. But what you do get can be in its own way as good.

Letters to Malcolm, ch. 5

And the joke, or tragedy, of it all is that these golden moments [of our past experience] which are so tormenting if we erect them into a norm, are entirely nourishing, wholesome, and enchanting if we are content to accept them for what they are, for memories. Properly bedded down in a past which we do not miserably try to conjure back, they will send up exquisite growths. Leave the bulbs alone, and the new flowers will come up. Grub them up and hope by fondling and sniffing, to get last year's blooms, and you will get nothing. 'Unless a seed die . . .'

Ibid.

Don't bother much about your feelings. When they are humble, loving, brave, give thanks for them; when they are conceited, selfish, cowardly, ask to have them altered. In neither case are they *you*, but only a thing that happens to you. What matters is your intentions and your behaviour.

Letters (13 June 1951)

'You all know,' said the Guide, 'that security is mortals' greatest enemy.'

The Pilgrim's Regress, bk 10, ch. 1

One is given strength to bear what happens to one, but not the 100 and 1 different things that *might* happen.

Unpublished letter (3 August 1956)

The practical problem of Christian politics is not that of drawing up schemes for a Christian society, but that of living as innocently as we can with unbelieving fellow-subjects under unbelieving rulers who will never be perfectly wise and good and who will sometimes be very wicked and very foolish.

'The Humanitarian Theory of Punishment',
Res Judicatae (June 1953)

Take the case of a sour old maid, who is a Christian, but cantankerous. On the other hand, take some pleasant and popular fellow, but who has never been to Church. Who knows how much more cantankerous the old maid might be is she were *not* a Christian, and how much more likeable the nice fellow might be if he *were* a Christian? You can't judge Christianity simply by comparing the *product* in those two people; you would need to know what kind of raw material Christ was working on in both cases.

Answers to Questions on Christianity

Some men's religion fails at the pinch: that of others does not appear to pluck up heart until the pinch comes.

English Literature in the Sixteenth Century, bk 2, sec. 1

A man knows that he has increased in virtue when he finds increased pleasure in virtuous acts.

Studies in Medieval and Renaissance Literature, ch. 4

'Here on the mountain I have spoken to you clearly: I will not often do so down in Narnia. Here on the mountain, the air is clear and your mind is clear; as you drop down into Narnia, the air will thicken. Take great care that it does not confuse your mind. And the signs which you have learned here will not look at all as you expect them to look, when you meet them there. That is why it is so important to know them by heart and pay no attention to appearances. Remember the signs and believe the signs. Nothing else matters. And now, daughter of Eve, farewell——'

The Silver Chair, ch. 2

The command, after all, was Take, eat: not Take, understand. Particularly, I hope I need not be tormented by the question 'What is this?'—this wafer, this sip of wine. That has a dreadful effect on me. It invites me to take 'this' out of its holy context and regard it as an object among objects, indeed as part of nature. It is like taking a red coal out of the fire to examine it: it becomes a dead coal.

Letters to Malcolm, ch. 19

Every virtue is a *habitus*—i.e. a *good* stock response.

'Christianity and Culture',
Christian Reflections

'The door into life generally opens behind us' and 'the only wisdom' for one 'haunted with the scent of unseen roses, is work'.* This secret fire goes out when you use the bellows: bank it down with what seems unlikely fuel of dogma and ethics, turn your back on it and attend to your duties, and then it will blaze.

The Problem of Pain, ch. 10

If a man who cannot draw horses is illustrating a book, the pictures that involve horses will be the bad pictures, let his spiritual condition be what it may.

The Allegory of Love, ch. 7, sec. 3

When Christianity tells you to feed the hungry it does not give you lessons in cookery. When it tells you to read the Scriptures it does not give you lessons in Hebrew and Greek, or even in English grammar. It was never intended to replace or supersede the ordinary human arts and sciences: it is rather a director which will set them all to the right jobs, and a source of energy which will give them all new life, if only they will put themselves at its disposal. . . .

The application of Christian principles, say, to trade unionism or education, must come from Christian trade unionists and Christian schoolmasters: just as Christian literature comes from Christian novelists and dramatists—not from the bench of bishops getting together and trying to write plays and novels in their spare time.

Mere Christianity, bk 3, ch. 3

God is not interested only in Christian writers as such. He is concerned with all kinds of writing. In the same way a sacred calling is not limited to ecclesiastical functions. The man who is weeding a field of turnips is also serving God.

'Heaven, Earth and Outer Space',
Decision (October 1963)

* George MacDonald.

I sometimes pray not for self-knowledge in general but for just so much self-knowledge at the moment as I can bear and use at the moment; the little daily dose.

Letters to Malcolm, ch. 6

God has not been trying an experiment on my faith or love in order to find out their quality. He knew it already. It was I who didn't. In this trial He makes us occupy the dock, the witness box, and the bench all at once. He always knew that my temple was a house of cards. His only way of making me realize the fact was to knock it down.

A Grief Observed, ch. 3

When he said, 'Be perfect,' He meant it. He meant that we must go in for the full treatment. It is hard; but the sort of compromise we are all hankering after is harder—in fact, it is impossible. It may be hard for an egg to turn into a bird; it would be a jolly sight harder for it to learn to fly while remaining an egg. We are like eggs at present. And you cannot go on indefinitely being just an ordinary decent egg. We must be hatched or go bad. . . .

If we let Him—for we can prevent Him, if we choose—He will make the feeblest and filthiest of us into a god or goddess, a dazzling, radiant, immortal creature, pulsating all through with such energy and joy and wisdom and love as we cannot now imagine, a bright stainless mirror which reflects back to God perfectly (though, of course, on a smaller scale) His own boundless power and delight and goodness. The process will be long and in parts very painful; but that is what we are in for. Nothing less.

Mere Christianity, bk 4, chs. 8, 9

If there lurks in most modern minds the notion that to desire our own good and earnestly to hope for the enjoyment of it is a bad thing, I submit that this notion has crept in from Kant and the Stoics and is no part of the Christian faith. Indeed, if we consider the unblushing promises of reward and the staggering nature of the rewards promised in the Gospels, it would seem that Our Lord finds our desires, not too strong, but too weak. We are half-hearted creatures, fooling about with drink and sex and ambition when infinite joy is offered us, like an ignorant child who wants to go on making mud pies in a slum because he cannot imagine what is meant by the offer of a holiday at the sea. . . . We are far too easily pleased.

We must not be troubled by unbelievers when they say that this promise of reward makes the Christian life a mercenary affair. There are different kinds of reward. There is the reward which has no natural connexion with the things you do to earn it, and is quite foreign to the desires that ought to accompany those things. Money is not the natural reward of love; that is why we call a man mercenary if he marries a woman for the sake of her money. But marriage is the proper reward for a real lover, and he is not mercenary for desiring it. A general who fights well in order to get a peerage is mercenary; a general who fights for victory is not, victory being the proper reward of battle as marriage is the proper reward of love. The proper rewards are not simply tacked on to the activity for which they are given, but are the activity itself in consummation.

Transposition and Other Addresses, ch. 2

VII

HELL AND HEAVEN

1. HELL

There is no neutral ground in the universe: every square inch, every split second, is claimed by God and counterclaimed by Satan.

'Christianity and Culture', *Christian Reflections*

But to a Christian the true tragedy of Nero must be not that he fiddled while the city was on fire but that he fiddled on the brink of hell. You must forgive me for the crude monosyllable. I know that many wiser and better Christians than I in these days do not like to mention heaven and hell even in a pulpit. I know, too, that nearly all the references to this subject in the New Testament come from a single source. But then that source is Our Lord Himself. People will tell you it is St. Paul, but that is untrue. These overwhelming doctrines are dominical. They are not really removable from the teaching of Christ or of His Church. If we do not believe them our presence in this church is great tomfoolery. If we do, we must sometime overcome our spiritual prudery and mention them.

Transposition and Other Addresses, ch. 4

God in His mercy made
The fixed pains of Hell.

'Divine Justice', *Poems*

Christianity asserts that every individual human being is

going to live for ever, and this must be either true or false. Now there are a good many things which would not be worth bothering about if I were going to live only seventy years, but which I had better bother about very seriously if I am going to live for ever. Perhaps my bad temper or my jealousy are gradually getting worse—so gradually that the increase in seventy years will not be very noticeable. But it might be absolute hell in a million years: in fact, if Christianity is true, Hell is the precisely correct technical term for what it would be.

Mere Christianity, bk 3, ch. 1

Picture to yourself a man who has risen to wealth or power by a continued course of treachery and cruelty, by exploiting for purely selfish ends the noble motions of his victims, laughing the while at their simplicity; who, having thus attained success, uses it for the gratification of lust and hatred and finally parts with the last rag of honour among thieves by betraying his own accomplices and jeering at their last moments of bewildered disillusionment. Suppose, further, that he does all this, not (as we like to imagine) tormented by remorse or even misgiving, but eating like a schoolboy and sleeping like a healthy infant—a jolly, ruddy-cheeked man, without a care in the world, unshakably confident to the very end that he alone has found the answer to the riddle of life, that God and man are fools whom he has got the better of, that his way of life is utterly successful, satisfactory, unassailable. . . . Supposing he *will* not be converted, what destiny in the eternal world can you regard as proper for him? . . . Even mercy can hardly wish to such a man his eternal, contented continuance in such ghastly illusion.

The Problem of Pain, ch. 8

'There are only two kinds of people in the end: those who say to God, "Thy will be done", and those to whom God says, in the end, "*Thy* will be done". All that are in Hell choose it.

Without that self-choice there could be no Hell. No soul that seriously and constantly desires joy will ever miss it.'

The Great Divorce, ch. 9

'There is always something they insist on keeping, even at the price of misery. There is always something they prefer to joy—that is, to reality.'

Ibid.

Be sure there is something inside you which, unless it is altered, will put it out of God's power to prevent your being eternally miserable. While that something remains there can be no Heaven for you, just as there can be no sweet smells for a man with a cold in the nose, and no music for a man who is deaf. It's not a question of God 'sending' us to Hell. In each of us there is something growing up which will of itself *be Hell* unless it is nipped in the bud. The matter is serious: let us put ourselves in His hands at once—this very day, this hour.

'The Trouble with "X" ',
Bristol Diocesan Gazette (August 1948)

Little by little, unconsciously, unintentionally, [a school matron] loosened the whole framework, blunted all the sharp edges, of my belief. The vagueness, the merely speculative character, of all this Occultism began to spread—yes, and to spread *deliciously*—to the stern truths of the creed. The whole thing became a matter of speculation: I was soon (in the famous words) 'altering "I believe" to "one does feel" '. And oh, the relief of it! . . . From the tyrannous noon of revelation I passed into the cool evening twilight of Higher Thought, where there was nothing to be obeyed, and nothing to be believed except what was either comforting or exciting. I do not mean that Miss C. did this; better say that the Enemy did this in me, taking occasion from things she innocently said.

Surprised by Joy, ch. 4

The Germans, perhaps, at first ill-treated the Jews because they hated them: afterwards they hated them much more because they had ill-treated them. The more cruel you are, the more you will hate; and the more you hate, the more cruel you will become—and so on in a vicious circle for ever.

Good and evil both increase at compound interest. That is why the little decisions you and I make every day are of such infinite importance. The smallest good act today is the capture of a strategic point from which, a few months later, you may be able to go on to victories you never dreamed of. An apparently trivial indulgence in lust or anger today is the loss of a ridge or railway line or bridgehead from which the enemy may launch an attack otherwise impossible.

Mere Christianity, bk 3, ch. 9

'The whole difficulty of understanding Hell is that the thing to be understood is so nearly Nothing. . . . it begins with a grumbling mood, and yourself still distinct from it: perhaps criticising it. And yourself, in a dark hour, may will that mood, embrace it. Ye can repent and come out of it again. But there may come a day when you can do that no longer. Then there will be no *you* left to criticise the mood, nor even to enjoy it, but just the grumble itself going on forever like a machine.'

The Great Divorce, ch. 9

'A damned soul is nearly nothing: it is shrunk, shut up in itself. Good beats upon the damned incessantly as sound waves beat on the ears of the deaf, but they cannot receive it. Their fists are clenched, their teeth are clenched, their eyes fast shut. First they will not, in the end they cannot, open their hands for gifts, or their mouths for food, or their eyes to see.'

Ibid., ch. 13

Put it more simply still. To be bad, he must exist and have intelligence and will. But existence, intelligence and will are in themselves good. Therefore he must be getting them from the Good Power: even to be bad he must borrow or steal from his opponent. And do you now begin to see why Christianity has always said that the devil is a fallen angel? That is not a mere story for the children. It is a real recognition of the fact that evil is a parasite, not an original thing. The powers which enable evil to carry on are powers given it by goodness. All the things which enable a bad man to be effectively bad are in themselves good things—resolution, cleverness, good looks, existence itself. That is why Dualism, in a strict sense, will not work.

Mere Christianity, bk 2, ch. 2

The forces which had begun, perhaps years ago, to eat away his humanity had now completed their work. The intoxicated will which had been slowly poisoning the intelligence and the affections had now at last poisoned itself and the whole psychic organism had fallen to pieces. Only a ghost was left—an everlasting unrest, a crumbling, a ruin, an odour of decay. 'And this,' thought Ransom, 'might be my destination.'

Perelandra, ch. 10

He had willed with his whole heart that there should be no reality and no truth, and now even the imminence of his own ruin could not wake him. . . . With eyes wide open, seeing that the endless terror is just about to begin and yet (for the moment) unable to feel terrified, he watches passively, not moving a finger for his own rescue, while the last links with joy and reason are severed, and drowsily sees the trap close upon his soul.

That Hideous Strength, ch. 16

The tempter always works on some *real* weakness in our own system of values: offers food to some need which we have starved.

'Equality', *The Spectator* (27 August 1943)

But we want a man hag-ridden by the Future—haunted by visions of an imminent heaven or hell upon earth. . . .

We want a whole race perpetually in pursuit of the rainbow's end, never honest, nor kind, nor happy *now*, but always using as mere fuel wherewith to heap the altar of the future every real gift which is offered them in the Present.

The Screwtape Letters, ch. 15

All the healthy and outgoing activities which we want him to avoid can be inhibited and *nothing* given in return, so that at last he may say, as one of my own patients said on his arrival down here, 'I now see that I spent most of my life in doing *neither* what I ought *nor* what I liked.'

Ibid., ch. 12

2. PAIN AND PLEASURE

'If God were good, He would wish to make His creatures perfectly happy, and if God were almighty He would be able to do what He wished. But the creatures are not happy. Therefore God lacks either goodness, or power, or both.' This is the problem of pain, in its simplest form. The possibility of answering it depends on showing that the terms 'good' and 'almighty', and perhaps also the term 'happy' are equivocal: for it must be admitted from the outset that if the popular meanings attached to these words are the best, or the only possible, meanings, then the argument is unanswerable.

The Problem of Pain, ch. 2

To ask whether the universe as we see it looks more like the work of a wise and good Creator or the work of chance, indifference, or malevolence, is to omit from the outset all the relevant factors in the religious problem. Christianity is not the conclusion of a philosophical debate on the origins of the universe: it is a catastrophic historical event following on the long spiritual preparation of humanity. . . . It is not a system into which we have to fit the awkward fact of pain: it is itself one of the awkward facts which have to be fitted into any system we make.

Ibid., ch. 1

God whispers to us in our pleasures, speaks in our conscience, but shouts in our pains: it is His megaphone to rouse a deaf world. A bad man, happy, is a man without the least inkling that his actions do not 'answer', that they are not in accord with the laws of the universe. . . .

Until the evil man finds evil unmistakably present in his existence, in the form of pain, he is enclosed in illusion. . . . No doubt Pain as God's megaphone is a terrible instrument: it may lead to final and unrepented rebellion. But it gives the only opportunity the bad man can have for amendment. It removes the veil; it plants the flag of truth within the fortress of a rebel soul.

Ibid., ch. 6

I believe that all pain is contrary to God's will, absolutely but not relatively. When I am taking a thorn out of my own finger (or a child's finger) the pain is 'absolutely' contrary to my will; i.e. if I could have chosen a situation without pain I would have done so. But I *do* will what caused the pain, relatively to the given situation; i.e. granted the thorn I prefer the pain to leaving the thorn where it is. A mother spanking a child would be in the same position; she would rather cause it this pain than let it go on pulling the cat's tail, but she would like it better if no situation which demands a smack had arisen.

Letters (31 January 1952)

I used to think it was a 'cruel' doctrine to say that troubles and sorrows were 'punishments'. But I find in practice that when you are in trouble, the moment you regard it as a 'punish-ment', it becomes easier to bear. If you think of this world as a place intended simply for our happiness, you find it quite intolerable: think of it as a place of training and correction and it's not so bad.

Answers to Questions on Christianity

The real problem is not why some humble, pious, believing people suffer, but why some do *not*. Our Lord Himself, it will be remembered, explained the salvation of those who are fortunate in this world only by referring to the unsearchable omnipotence of God.

The Problem of Pain, ch. 6

I am progressing along the path of life in my ordinary con-tentedly fallen and godless condition, absorbed in a merry meeting with my friends for the morrow or a bit of work that tickles my vanity to-day, a holiday or a new book, when suddenly a stab of abdominal pain that threatens serious disease, or a headline in the newspapers that threatens us all with destruction, sends this whole pack of cards tumbling down. At first I am overwhelmed, and all my little happinesses look like broken toys. . . . And perhaps, by God's grace, I succeed, and for a day or two become a creature consciously dependent on God and drawing its strength from the right sources. But the moment the threat is withdrawn, my whole nature leaps back to the toys. . . . Thus the terrible necessity of tribulation is only too clear. God has had me for but forty-eight hours and then only by dint of taking everything else away from me. Let Him but sheathe that sword for a moment and I behave like a puppy when the hated bath is over—I shake myself as dry as I can and race off to reacquire my comfortable dirtiness, if not in the nearest manure heap, at least in the nearest flower bed. And that is why tribulations cannot cease until God either sees us remade or sees that our remaking is now hopeless.   *Ibid.*

To how few of us He *dare* send happiness because He knows we will forget Him if He gives us any sort of nice things for the moment.

Letters (5 March 1951)

I have no doubt at all that pleasure is in itself a good and pain in itself an evil; if not, then the whole Christian tradition about heaven and hell and the passion of our Lord seems to have no meaning. Pleasure, then, is good; a 'sinful' pleasure means a good offered, and accepted, under conditions which involve a breach of the moral law.

'Christianity and Culture', *Christian Reflections*

The settled happiness and security which we all desire, God withholds from us by the very nature of the world: but joy, pleasure, and merriment, He has scattered broadcast. We are never safe, but we have plenty of fun, and some ecstasy. It is not hard to see why. The security we crave would teach us to rest our hearts in this world and oppose an obstacle to our return to God: a few moments of happy love, a landscape, a symphony, a merry meeting with our friends, a bathe or a football match, have no such tendency. Our Father refreshes us on the journey with some pleasant inns, but will not encourage us to mistake them for home.

The Problem of Pain, ch. 7

Pleasure, pushed to its extreme, shatters us like pain.... When natural things look most divine, the demoniac is just round the corner.

The Four Loves, ch. 5

One can concentrate on the pleasure as an event in one's own nervous system—subjectify it—and ignore the smell of Deity that hangs about it.

Letters to Malcolm, ch. 17

He made the pleasures: all our research so far has not enabled us to produce one. All we can do is to encourage the humans to take the pleasures which our Enemy has produced, at times, or in ways, or in degrees, which He has forbidden. Hence we always try to work away from the natural condition of any pleasure to that in which it is least natural, least redolent of its Maker, and least pleasurable. An ever increasing craving for an ever diminishing pleasure is the formula.

The Screwtape Letters, ch. 9

But aren't there bad, unlawful pleasures? Certainly there are. But in calling them 'bad pleasures' I take it we are using a kind of shorthand. We mean 'pleasures snatched by unlawful acts'. It is the stealing of the apple that is bad, not the sweetness. The sweetness is still a beam from the glory. That does not palliate the stealing. It makes it worse. There is sacrilege in the theft. We have abused a holy thing.

Letters to Malcolm, ch. 17

3. HEAVEN

Servile fear is, to be sure, the lowest form of religion. But a god such that there could never be occasion for even servile fear, a *safe* god, a tame god, soon proclaims himself to any sound mind as a fantasy. I have met no people who fully disbelieved in Hell and also had a living and life-giving belief in Heaven.

Letters to Malcolm, ch. 14

If you read history you will find that the Christians who did most for the present world were just those who thought most of the next. The Apostles themselves, who set on foot the conversion of the Roman Empire, the great men who built up the Middle Ages, the English Evangelicals who abolished the Slave Trade, all left their mark on Earth, precisely because their minds were occupied with Heaven. It is since Christians have largely ceased to think of the other world that they have become so ineffective in this. Aim at Heaven and you will get earth 'thrown in'; aim at earth and you will get neither.

Mere Christianity, bk 3, ch. 10

If we insist on keeping Hell (or even earth) we shall not see Heaven: if we accept Heaven we shall not be able to retain even the smallest and most intimate souvenirs of Hell. I believe, to be sure, that any man who reaches Heaven will find that what he abandoned (even in plucking out his right eye) was precisely nothing: that the kernel of what he was really seeking even in his most depraved wishes will be there, beyond expectation, waiting for him in 'the High Countries'. . . .

I think earth, if chosen instead of Heaven, will turn out to have been, all along, only a region in Hell: and earth, if put second to Heaven, to have been from the beginning a part of Heaven itself.

Preface to *The Great Divorce*

I had recently come to know an old, dirty, gabbling, tragic, Irish parson who had long since lost his faith but retained his living. By the time I met him his only interest was the search for evidence of 'human survival'. On this he read and talked incessantly, and, having a highly critical mind, could never satisfy himself. What was especially shocking was that the ravenous desire for personal immortality co-existed in him with (apparently) a total indifference to all that could, on a sane view, make immortality desirable. He was not seeking the Beatific Vision and did not even believe in God. . . . All he wanted was the assurance that something he could call 'himself' would, on almost any terms, last longer than his bodily life. . . . And his state of mind appeared to me the most contemptible I had ever encountered.

Surprised by Joy, ch. 13

There is no need to be worried by facetious people who try to make the Christian hope of 'heaven' ridiculous by saying they do not want 'to spend eternity playing harps'. The answer to such people is that if they cannot understand books written for grown-ups, they should not talk about them. All the scriptural imagery (harps, crowns, gold, etc.) is, of course, a merely symbolical attempt to express the inexpressible. Musical instruments are mentioned because for many people (not all) music is the thing known in the present life which most strongly suggests ecstasy and infinity. Crowns are mentioned to suggest the fact that those who are united with God in eternity share His splendour and power and joy. Gold is mentioned to suggest the timelessness of Heaven (gold does not rust) and the preciousness of it. People who take these symbols literally might as well think that when Christ told us to be like doves, He meant that we were to lay eggs.

Mere Christianity, bk 3, ch. 10

We are afraid that heaven is a bribe, and that if we make it our goal we shall no longer be disinterested. It is not so. Heaven offers nothing that a mercenary soul can desire. It is safe to tell the pure in heart that they shall see God, for only the pure in heart want to. There are rewards that do not sully motives. A man's love for a woman is not mercenary because he wants to marry her, nor his love for poetry mercenary because he wants to read it, nor his love of exercise less disinterested because he wants to run and leap and walk. Love, by definition, seeks to enjoy its object.

The Problem of Pain, ch. 10

My grandfather, I'm told, used to say that he 'looked forward to having some very interesting conversations with St. Paul when he got to heaven'. Two clerical gentlemen talking at ease in a club! It never seemed to cross his mind that an encounter with St. Paul might be rather an overwhelming experience even for an Evangelical clergyman of good family. But when Dante saw the great apostles in heaven they affected him like *mountains*. There's lots to be said against devotions to saints; but at least they keep on reminding us that we are very small people compared with them. How much smaller before their Master?

Letters to Malcolm, ch. 2

Personality is eternal and inviolable. But then, personality is not a datum from which we start. The individualism in which we all begin is only a parody or shadow of it. True personality lies ahead—how far ahead, for most of us, I dare not say. And the key to it does not lie in ourselves. It will not be attained by development from within outwards. It will come to us when we occupy those places in the structure of the eternal cosmos for which we were designed or invented. As a colour first reveals its true quality when placed by an excellent artist in its pre-elected spot between certain others, as a spice reveals its true flavour when inserted just where and when a good cook wishes among the other ingredients, as the dog becomes really doggy only when he has taken his place in the household of man, so we shall then first be true persons when we have suffered ourselves to be fitted into our places. We are marble waiting to be shaped, metal waiting to be run into a mould. . . .

We shall be true and everlasting and really divine persons only in Heaven, just as we are, even now, coloured bodies only in the light.

Transposition and Other Addresses, ch. 3

Most of man's psychological make-up is probably due to his body: when his body dies all that will fall off him, and the real central man, the thing that chose, that made the best or the worst out of this material, will stand naked. All sorts of nice things which we thought our own. but which were really due to a good digestion, will fall off some of us; all sorts of nasty things which were due to complexes or bad health will fall off others. We shall then, for the first time, see every one as he really was. There will be surprises.

Mere Christianity, bk 3, ch. 4

I can imagine someone saying that he dislikes my idea of heaven as a place where we are patted on the back. But proud misunderstanding is behind that dislike. In the end that Face which is the delight or the terror of the universe must be turned upon each of us either with one expression or with the other, either conferring glory inexpressible or inflicting shame that can never be cured or disguised. .... It is written that we shall 'stand before' Him, shall appear, shall be inspected. The promise of glory is the promise, almost incredible and only possible by the work of Christ, that some of us, that any of us who really chooses, shall actually survive that examination, shall find approval, shall please God. To please God ... to be a real ingredient in the divine happiness ... to be loved by God, not merely pitied, but delighted in as an artist delights in his work or a father in a son—it seems impossible, a weight or burden of glory which our thoughts can hardly sustain. But so it is.

Transposition and Other Addresses, ch. 2

Heaven is, by definition, outside our experience, but all intelligible descriptions must be of things within our experience. The scriptural picture of heaven is therefore just as symbolical as the picture which our desire, unaided, invents for itself; heaven is not really full of jewelry any more than it is really the beauty of Nature, or a fine piece of music. The difference is that the scriptural imagery has authority. It comes to us from writers who were closer to God than we, and it has stood the test of Christian experience down the centuries.

Ibid.

We do not want merely to *see* beauty, though, God knows, even that is bounty enough. We want something else which can hardly be put into words—to be united with the beauty we see, to pass into it, to receive it into ourselves, to bathe in it, to become part of it. That is why we have peopled air and earth and water with gods and goddesses and nymphs and elves— that, though we cannot, yet these projections can, enjoy in themselves that beauty, grace, and power of which Nature is the image. That is why the poets tell us such lovely falsehoods. They talk as if the west wind could really sweep into a human soul; but it can't. They tell us that 'beauty born of murmuring sound' will pass into a human face; but it won't. Or not yet. For if we take the imagery of Scripture seriously, if we believe that God will one day *give* us the Morning Star and cause us to *put on* the splendour of the sun, then we may surmise that both the ancient myths and the modern poetry, so false as history, may be very near the truth as prophecy. At present we are on the outside of the world, the wrong side of the door. We discern the freshness and purity of morning, but they do not make us fresh and pure. We cannot mingle with the splendours we see. But all the leaves of the New Testament are rustling with the rumour that it will not always be so. Some day, God willing, we shall get *in*.

Ibid.

'The further up and the further in you go, the bigger everything gets. The inside is larger than the outside.'

The Last Battle, ch. 16

At present we tend to think of the soul as somehow 'inside' the body. But the glorified body of the resurrection as I conceive it—the sensuous life raised from its death—will be inside the soul. As God is not in space but space is in God.

Letters to Malcolm, ch. 20

To enter heaven is to become more human than you ever succeeded in being in earth; to enter hell, is to be banished from humanity. What is cast (or casts itself) into hell is not a man: it is 'remains'. To be a complete man means to have the passions obedient to the will and the will offered to God. . . .

We know much more about heaven than hell, for heaven is the home of humanity and therefore contains all that is implied in a glorified human life: but hell was not made for men. It is in no sense *parallel* to heaven: it is 'the darkness outside', the outer rim where being fades away into nonentity. . . .

I willingly believe that the damned are, in one sense, success-ful, rebels to the end; that the doors of hell are locked on the *inside*. . . .

In the long run the answer to all those who object to the doctrine of hell, is itself a question: 'What are you asking God to do?' To wipe out their past sins and, at all costs, to give them a fresh start, smoothing every difficulty and offering every miraculous help? But He has done so, on Calvary. To forgive them? They will not be forgiven. To leave them alone? Alas, I am afraid that is what He does.

The Problem of Pain, ch. 8

If grace perfects nature it must expand all our natures into the full richness of the diversity which God intended when He made them, and Heaven will display far more variety than Hell. 'One fold' doesn't mean 'one pool'. Cultivated roses and daffodils are no more alike than wild roses and daffodils.

Letters to Malcolm, ch. 2

Matter enters our experience only by becoming sensation (when we perceive it) or conception (when we understand it). That is, by becoming soul. That element in the soul which it becomes will, in my view, be raised and glorified; the hills and valleys of Heaven will be to those you now experience not as a copy is to an original, nor as a substitute is to the genuine article, but as the flower to the root, or the diamond to the coal. It will be eternally true that they originated with matter;

let us therefore bless matter. But in entering our soul as alone it can enter—that is, by being perceived and known—matter has turned into soul (like the Undines who acquired a soul by marriage with a mortal).

Ibid., ch. 22

It is said 'To him that overcometh I will give a white stone, and in the stone a new name written, which no man knoweth saving he that receiveth it'. What can be more a man's own than this new name which even in eternity remains a secret between God and him? And what shall we take this secrecy to mean? Surely, that each of the redeemed shall forever know and praise some one aspect of the divine beauty better than any other creature can. Why else were individuals created, but that God, loving all infinitely, should love each differently? And this difference, so far from impairing, floods with meaning the love of all blessed creatures for one another, the communion of the saints. If all experienced God in the same way and returned Him an identical worship, the song of the Church triumphant would have no symphony, it would be like an orchestra in which all the instruments played the same note.... For doubtless the continually successful, yet never completed, attempt by each soul to communicate its unique vision to all others (and that by means whereof earthly art and philosophy are but clumsy imitations) is also among the ends for which the individual was created.

The Problem of Pain, ch. 10

When we see the face of God we shall know that we have always known it. He has been a party to, has made, sustained and moved moment by moment within, all our earthly experiences of innocent love. All that was true love in them was, even on earth, far more His than ours, and ours only because His. In Heaven there will be no anguish and no duty of turning away from our earthly Beloveds. First, because we shall have turned already; from the portraits to the Original, from the rivulets to the Fountain, from the creatures He made lovable to Love Himself. But secondly, because we shall find them all in Him. By loving Him more than them we shall love them more than we now do.

The Four Loves, ch. 6

'Hell is a state of mind—ye never said a truer word. And every state of mind, left to itself, every shutting up of the creature within the dungeon of its own mind—is, in the end, Hell. But Heaven is not a state of mind. Heaven is reality itself. All that is fully real is Heavenly.'

The Great Divorce, ch. 9

Nature is mortal; we shall outlive her. When all the suns and nebulae have passed away, each one of you will still be alive. Nature is only the image, the symbol; but it is the symbol Scripture invites me to use. We are summoned to pass in through Nature, beyond her, into that splendour which she fitfully reflects.

And in there, in beyond Nature, we shall eat of the tree of life. At present, if we are reborn in Christ, the spirit in us lives directly on God; but the mind, and still more the body, receives life from Him at a thousand removes—through our ancestors, through our food, through the elements. The faint, far-off results of those energies which God's creative rapture implanted in matter when He made the worlds are what we now call physical pleasures; and even thus filtered, they are too much for our present management. What would it be to taste at the fountain-head that stream of which even these lower reaches prove so intoxicating? Yet that, I believe, is what lies before us. The whole man is to drink joy from the fountain of joy. As St. Augustine said, the rapture of the saved soul will 'flow over' into the glorified body. In the light of our present specialized and depraved appetites we cannot imagine this *torrens voluptatis,* and I warn everyone most seriously not to try. But it must be mentioned, to drive out thoughts even more misleading— thoughts that what is saved is a mere ghost, or that the risen body lives in numb insensibility.

Transposition and Other Addresses, ch. 2

He saw not only Them; he saw Him. This animal, this thing begotten in a bed, could look on Him. What is blinding, suffocating fire to you, is now cool light to him, is clarity itself, and wears the form of a Man.

The Screwtape Letters, ch. 31

Then the new earth and sky, the same yet not the same as these, will rise in us as we have risen in Christ. And once again, after who knows what aeons of the silence and the dark, the birds will sing and the waters flow, and lights and shadows move across the hills, and the faces of our friends laugh upon us with amazed recognition.

Guesses, of course, only guesses. If they are not true, some- thing better will be. For 'we know that we shall be made like Him, for we shall see Him as He is'.

Letters to Malcolm, ch. 22

Think of yourself just as a seed patiently wintering in the earth; waiting to come up a flower in the Gardener's good time, up into the *real* world, the real waking. I suppose that our whole present life, looked back on from there, will seem only a drowsy half-waking. We are here in the land of dreams. But cock-crow is coming. It is nearer now than when I began this letter.

Unpublished letter (28 June 1963)

And then, of her [his deceased wife], and of every created thing I praise, I should say 'In some way, in its unique way, like Him who made it'.

Thus up from the garden to the Gardener, from the sword to the Smith. To the life-giving Life and the Beauty that makes beautiful.

'She is in God's hand.' That gains a new energy when I think of her as a sword. Perhaps the earthly life I shared with her was only part of the tempering. Now perhaps He grasps the hilt; weighs the new weapon; makes lightnings with it in the air. 'A right Jerusalem blade.'

A Grief Observed, ch. 4

Oh, thou that art unwearying, that dost neither sleep
  Nor slumber, who didst take
All care for Lazarus in the careless tomb, oh keep
  Watch for me till I wake.

'The Naked Seed', *Poems*

'There *was* a real railway accident,' said Aslan softly. 'Your father and mother and all of you are—as you used to call it in the Shadow-Lands—dead. The term is over: the holidays have begun. The dream is ended: this is the morning.'

And as He spoke He no longer looked to them like a lion; but the things that began to happen after that were so great and beautiful that I cannot write them. And for us this is the end of all the stories, and we can most truly say that they all lived happily ever after. But for them it was only the beginning of the real story. All their life in this world and all their adventures in Narnia had only been the cover and the title page: now at last they were beginning Chapter One of the Great Story, which no one on earth has read: which goes on for ever: in which every chapter is better than the one before.

The Last Battle, ch. 16

VIII

LOVE AND SEX

1. AFFECTION AND FRIENDSHIP

I do not for a moment question that Affection is responsible for nine-tenths of whatever solid and durable happiness there is in our natural lives.

The Four Loves, ch. 3

Affection is the humblest love. It gives itself no airs. People can be proud of being 'in love', or of friendship. Affection is modest—even furtive and shame-faced. Once when I had remarked on the affection quite often found between cat and dog, my friend replied, 'Yes. But I bet no dog would ever confess it to the other dogs.' That is at least a good caricature of much human Affection. . . . Affection almost slinks or seeps through our lives. It lives with humble, un-dress, private things; soft slippers, old clothes, old jokes, the thump of a sleepy dog's tail on the kitchen floor, the sound of a sewing machine, a gollywog left on the lawn.

Ibid.

The moment when one first says, really meaning it, that though he is not 'my sort of man' he is a very good man 'in his own way' is one of liberation. It does not feel like that; we may feel only tolerant and indulgent. But really we have crossed a frontier. That 'in his own way' means that we are getting beyond our own idiosyncrasies, that we are learning to appreciate goodness or intelligence in themselves, not merely goodness or intelligence flavoured and served to suit our own palate.

'Dogs and cats should always be brought up together,' said someone, 'it broadens their minds so.' Affection broadens ours.

Ibid.

We picture lovers face to face but Friends side by side; their eyes look ahead.

That is why those pathetic people who simply 'want friends' can never make any. The very condition of having Friends is that we should want something else besides Friends. Where the truthful answer to the question *Do you see the same truth?* would be 'I see nothing and I don't care about the truth; I only want a Friend', no Friendship can arise.

Ibid., ch. 4

The First is the *alter ego*, the man who first reveals to you that you are not alone in the world by turning out (beyond hope) to share all your most secret delights. There is nothing to be overcome in making him your friend; he and you join like rain-drops on a window. But the Second Friend is the man who disagrees with you about everything. He is not so much the *alter ego* as the anti-self. Of course he shares your interests; otherwise he would not become your friend at all. But he has approached them all at a different angle. He has read all the right books but has got the wrong thing out of every one. It is as if he spoke your language but mispronounced it. How can he be so nearly right and yet, invariably, just not right? He is as fascinating (and infuriating) as a woman.

Surprised by Joy, ch. 13

Nothing, I suspect, is more astonishing in any man's life than the discovery that there do exist people very, very like himself.

Ibid., ch. 8

2. LOVE

If I am sure of anything I am sure that His teaching was never meant to confirm my congenital preference for safe investments and limited liabilities. . . .

Love anything, and your heart will certainly be wrung and possibly be broken. If you want to make sure of keeping it intact, you must give your heart to no one, not even to an animal. Wrap it carefully round with hobbies and little luxuries; avoid all entanglements; lock it up safe in the casket or coffin of your selfishness. But in that casket—safe, dark, motionless, airless—it will change. It will not be broken; it will become unbreakable, impenetrable, irredeemable. The alternative to tragedy, or at least to the risk of tragedy, is damnation. The only place outside Heaven where you can be perfectly safe from all the dangers and perturbations of love is Hell.

I believe that the most lawless and inordinate loves are less contrary to God's will than a self-invited and self-protective lovelessness.

The Four Loves, ch. 6

All natural affections can become rivals to spiritual love: but they can also be preparatory imitations of it, training (so to speak) of the spiritual muscles which Grace may later put to a higher service; as women nurse dolls in childhood and later nurse children. There may come an occasion for renouncing this love; pluck out your right eye. But you need to have an eye first: a creature which had none—which had only got so far as a 'photo-sensitive' spot—would be very ill employed in meditation on that severe text.

Ibid., ch. 2

'You cannot love a fellow-creature fully till you love God.'
The Great Divorce, ch. 11

It is probably impossible to love any human being simply 'too much'. We may love him too much *in proportion* to our love for God; but it is the smallness of our love for God, not the greatness of our love for the man, that constitutes the inordinacy.

The Four Loves, ch. 6

Have you read *Esmond* lately? What a detestable woman is Lady Castlewood: and yet I believe Thackeray means us to like her, on the ground that all her actions spring from 'love'. This love is, in his language, 'pure'—i.e., it is not promiscuous or sensual. It is none the less a wholly uncorrected natural passion, idolatrous and insatiable. Was that the great 19th century heresy—that 'pure' or 'noble' passions didn't need to be crucified and re-born, but could of themselves lead to happiness? Yet one sees it makes Lady C. disastrous both as a wife and a mother, and is a source of misery to herself and all whom she meets.

Letters (*c*. January 1942)

Need-love cries to God from our poverty; Gift-love longs to serve, or even to suffer for, God; Appreciative love says: 'We give thanks to thee for thy great glory.' Need-love says of a woman 'I cannot live without her'; Gift-love longs to give her happiness, comfort, protection—if possible, wealth; Appreciative love gazes and holds its breath and is silent, rejoices that such a wonder should exist even if not for him, will not be wholly dejected by losing her, would rather have it so than never to have seen her at all.

The Four Loves, ch. 2

3. SEX

We use a most unfortunate idiom when we say of a lustful man prowling the streets, that he 'wants a woman'. Strictly speaking, a woman is just what he does not want. He wants a pleasure for which a woman happens to be the necessary piece of apparatus. ... Now Eros makes a man really want, not a woman, but one particular woman. In some mysterious but quite indisputable fashion the lover desires the Beloved herself, not the pleasure she can give.

Ibid., ch. 5

The monstrosity of sexual intercourse outside marriage is that those who indulge in it are trying to isolate one kind of union (the sexual) from all the other kinds of union which were intended to go along with it and make up the total union. The Christian attitude does not mean that there is anything wrong about sexual pleasure, any more than about the pleasure of eating. It means that you must not isolate that pleasure and try to get it by itself, any more than you ought to try to get the pleasures of taste without swallowing and digesting, by chewing things and spitting them out again.

Mere Christianity, bk 3, ch. 6

We have been told, till one is sick of hearing it, that sexual desire is in the same state as any of our other natural desires and that if only we abandon the silly old Victorian idea of hushing it up, everything in the garden will be lovely. It is not true. The moment you look at the facts, and away from the propaganda, you see that it is not.

Ibid., bk 3, ch. 5

When I was a youngster, all the progressive people were saying, 'Why all this prudery? Let us treat sex just as we treat all our other impulses.' I was simple-minded enough to believe they meant what they said. I have since discovered that they meant exactly the opposite. They meant that sex was to be treated as no other impulse in our nature has ever been treated by civilized people. All the others, we admit, have to be bridled. . . . But every unkindness and breach of faith seems to be condoned provided that the object aimed at is 'four bare legs in a bed'.

It is like having a morality in which stealing fruit is considered wrong—unless you steal nectarines. . . .

If I object to boys who steal my nectarines, must I be supposed to disapprove of nectarines in general? Or even of boys in general? It might, you know, be stealing that I disapproved of.

'We Have No "Right to Happiness"',
The Saturday Evening Post
(21–28 December 1963)

It becomes clear that humanity has some motive other than concealment for comparing erotic experience to gardens and flowers: that the erotic experience, thus compared, becomes somehow more interesting—that it is borrowing attractiveness from the flowers, not they from it. And this situation is very common. Donne, in elegies which express quite frankly the most ravenous and unidealised appetite, yet finds that he can improve his poem by comparing his mistress to the earth or to a landscape. Burns tells us that his love is like a red, red rose. These phenomena which might, in a confused glance, be taken to support the Freudian view, are really its refutation.

They Asked for a Paper, ch. 7

Chastity is the most unpopular of the Christian virtues. There is no getting away from it: the old Christian rule is, 'Either marriage, with complete faithfulness to your partner, or else total abstinence'. Now this is so difficult and so contrary to our instincts, that obviously either Christianity is wrong or our sexual instinct, as it now is, has gone wrong. One or the other. . . .

You can get a large audience together for a strip-tease act—that is, to watch a girl undress on the stage. Now suppose you came to a country where you could fill a theatre by simply bringing a covered plate on to the stage and then slowly lifting the cover so as to let every one see, just before the lights went out, that it contained a mutton chop or a bit of bacon, would you not think that in that country something had gone wrong with the appetite for food? And would not anyone who had grown up in a different world think there was something equally queer about the state of the sex instinct among us?

Mere Christianity, bk 3, ch. 5

There have been very few societies ... in which it was considered shameful to make a drawing of the naked human body: a detailed unexpurgated drawing which omits nothing that the eye can see. On the other hand, there have been very few societies in which it would have been permissible to give an equally detailed description of the same object in words. What is the cause of this seemingly arbitrary discrimination? ...

Sit down and draw your nude. When you have finished it, take your pen and attempt the written description. Before you have finished you will be faced with a problem which simply did not exist while you were working at the picture. When you come to those parts of the body which are not usually mentioned, you will have to make a choice of vocabulary. And you will find that you have only four alternatives: a nursery word, an archaism, a word from the gutter, or a scientific word. You will not find any ordinary, neutral word comparable to 'hand' or 'nose'. . . . Language forces you to an explicit comment. . . . I am talking of course, about mere draughtsmanship at its simplest level.

'Prudery and Philology', *The Spectator*
(21 January 1965)

It is not for nothing that every language and literature in the world is full of jokes about sex. Many of them may be dull or disgusting and nearly all of them are old. But we must insist that they embody an attitude to Venus which in the long run endangers the Christian life far less than a reverential gravity. We must not attempt to find an absolute in the flesh. Banish play and laughter from the bed of love and you may let in a false goddess. . . . We are under no obligation at all to sing all our love-duets in the throbbing world-without-end, heart-breaking manner of Tristan and Isolde; let us often sing like Papageno and Papagena instead.

The Four Loves, ch. 5

By the words 'unaesthetic womanhood' I think [Charles] Williams means to direct our thoughts to something which is really characteristic of the feminine mind—that monopolistic concentration, for good or ill, on the dominant idea, which brings it about that in a woman good states of mind are un-weakened and undissipated, or bad states of mind unrelieved, by fancy and speculation and mere drifting. Hence that tenacity both of good and evil, those chemically pure states of devotion or of egoism, which are hardly conceivable in my own sex. The lady in Mr. Eliot's poem who said 'How you digress' was speaking for all women to all men.

Arthurian Torso, pt 2, ch. 5

The effects of the Fall on [Adam in *Paradise Lost*] are quite unlike its effects on the woman. She had rushed at once into false sentiment which made murder itself appear a proof of fine sensibility. Adam, after eating the fruit, goes in the opposite direction. He becomes a man of the world, a punster, an aspirant to fine raillery. He compliments Eve on her palate and says the real weakness of Paradise is that there were too few forbidden trees. The father of all the bright epigrammatic wasters and the mother of all the corrupting female novelists are now both before us. As critics have pointed out, Adam and Eve 'become human' at this point.

A Preface to 'Paradise Lost', ch. 18

A society in which conjugal infidelity is tolerated must always be in the long run a society adverse to women. Women ... are more naturally monogamous than men; it is a biological necessity. Where promiscuity prevails, they will therefore always be more often the victims than the culprits. Also, domestic happiness is more necessary to them than to us. ... Thus in the ruthless war of promiscuity women are at a double disadvantage. They play for higher stakes and are also more likely to lose.

'We Have No "Right to Happiness"',
The Saturday Evening Post (21–28 December 1963)

[In feudal society] marriages had nothing to do with love, and no 'nonsense' about marriage was tolerated. All matches were matches of interest, and, worse still, of an interest that was continually changing. When the alliance which had answered would answer no longer, the husband's object was to get rid of the lady as quickly as possible. ... The same woman who was the lady and 'the dearest dread' of her vassals was often little better than a piece of property to her husband. ... Any idealization of sexual love, in a society where marriage is purely utilitarian, must begin by being an idealization of adultery.

The Allegory of Love, ch. 1, sec. 1

There is, hidden or flaunted, a sword between the sexes till an entire marriage reconciles them. It is arrogance in us to call frankness, fairness, and chivalry 'masculine' when we see them in a woman; it is arrogance in them, to describe a man's sensitiveness or tact or tenderness as 'feminine'. But also what poor, warped fragments of humanity most mere men and mere women must be to make the implications of that arrogance plausible. Marriage heals this. Jointly the two become fully human 'In the image of God created He *them*'. Thus, by a paradox, this carnival of sexuality leads us out beyond our sexes.

A Grief Observed, ch. 3

One of the ends for which sex was created was to symbolize to us the hidden things of God. One of the functions of human marriage is to express the nature of the union between Christ and the Church.

'Notes on the Way', *Time and Tide*
(14 August 1948)

Being in love is a good thing, but it is not the best thing. There are many things below it, but there are also things above it. You cannot make it the basis of a whole life. It is a noble feeling, but it is still a feeling. . . . Who could bear to live in that excitement for even five years? . . . But, of course, ceasing to be 'in love' need not mean ceasing to love. Love in a second sense—love as distinct from 'being in love' is not merely a feeling. It is a deep unity, maintained by the will and deliberately strengthened by habit; reinforced by (in Christian marriages) the grace which both parents ask, and receive, from God. They can have this love for each other even at those moments when they do not like each other; as you love yourself even when you do not like yourself. They can retain this love even when each would easily, if they allowed themselves, be 'in love' with someone else. 'Being in love' first moved them to promise fidelity: this quieter love enables them to keep the promise. It is on this love that the engine of marriage is run; being in love was the explosion that started it.

Mere Christianity, bk 3, ch. 6

People get from books the idea that if you have married the right person you may expect to go on 'being in love' for ever. As a result, when they find they are not, they think this proves they have made a mistake and are entitled to a change—not realising that, when they have changed, the glamour will presently go out of the new love just as it went out of the old one. In this department of life, as in every other, thrills come at the beginning and do not last. . . .

Let the thrill go—let it die away—go on through that period of death into the quieter interest and happiness that follow—and you will find you are living in a world of new thrills all the time. But if you decide to make thrills your regular diet and try to prolong them artificially, they will all get weaker and weaker. and fewer and fewer, and you will be a bored, disillusioned old man for the rest of your life. It is because so few people understand this that you find many middle-aged men and women maundering about their lost youth, at the very age when new horizons ought to be appearing and new doors opening all round them. It is much better fun to learn to swim than to go on endlessly (and hopelessly) trying to get back the feeling you had when you first went paddling as a small boy.

Ibid.

IX

NATURE

1. THE REALITY OF NATURE

There is a dignity and poignancy in the bare fact that a thing exists.

They Asked for a Paper, ch. 9

Surprised he stood
To feel that wideness quenching his hot mood,
Then shouted, 'Trembling darkness, trembling green,
What do you mean, wild wood, what do you mean?'

Dymer, canto 1, st. 19

Medicine labours to restore 'natural' structure or 'normal' function. But greed, egoism, self-deception and self-pity are not unnatural or abnormal in the same sense as astigmatism or a floating kidney. For who, in Heaven's name, would describe as natural or normal the man from whom these failings were wholly absent? 'Natural,' if you like, in a quite different sense; archnatural, unfallen. We have seen only one such Man. And He was not at all like the psychologist's picture of the integrated, balanced, adjusted, happily married, employed, popular citizen. You can't really be very well 'adjusted' to your world if it says you 'have a devil' and ends by nailing you up naked to a stake of wood.

The Four Loves, ch. 3

All the beauty [of Nature] withers when we try to make it an absolute. Put first things first and we get second things thrown in: put second things first and we lose *both* first and second things. We never get, say, even the sensual pleasure of food at its best when we are being greedy.

Letters (23 April 1951)

In space and time there is no such thing as an organism, there are only animals and vegetables. There are no mere vegetables, only trees, flowers, turnips, &c. There are no 'trees', except beeches, elms, oaks, and the rest. There is even no such thing as 'an elm'. There is only *this* elm, in such a year of its age at such an hour of the day, thus lighted, thus moving, thus acted on by all the past and all the present, and affording such and such experiences to me and my dog and the insect on its trunk and the man a thousand miles away who is remembering it. A real elm, in fact, can be uttered only by a poem.

The Personal Heresy, ch. 5

No one sunrise has ever been exactly like another. Take away from the sunrises that in which they differ and what is left will be identical. Such abstracted identicals are what science predicts. But life as we live it is not reducible to such identities. Every real physical event, much more every human experience, has behind it, in the long run, the whole previous history of the real universe—which is not itself an 'instance' of anything—and is therefore always festooned with those particularities which science for her own purposes quite rightly discounts. Doesn't the whole art of contriving a good experiment consist in devising means whereby the irrelevancies— that is, the historical particularities—can be reduced to the minimum?

Letters to Malcolm, ch. 7

Nature is by human (and probably by Divine) standards partly good and partly evil. We Christians believe that she has been corrupted. But the same tang or flavour runs through both her corruptions and her excellences. Everything is in character. . . . The evils we see in Nature are, so to speak, the evils proper to *this* Nature. Her very character decreed that if she were corrupted the corruption would take this form and not another. The horrors of parasitism and the glories of motherhood are good and evil worked out of the same basic theme or idea.

Miracles, ch. 9

If you take nature as a teacher she will teach you exactly the lessons you had already decided to learn; this is only another way of saying that nature does not teach. The tendency to take her as a teacher is obviously very easily grafted on to the experience we call 'love of nature'. But it is only a graft. While we are actually subjected to them, the 'moods' and 'spirits' of nature point no morals. Overwhelming gaiety, insupportable grandeur, sombre desolation are flung at you. Make what you can of them, if you must make at all. The only imperative that nature utters is, 'Look. Listen. Attend.' . . .

A true philosophy may sometimes validate an experience of nature; an experience of nature cannot validate a philosophy.

The Four Loves, ch. 2

Nature never taught me that there exists a God of glory and of infinite majesty. I had to learn that in other ways. But nature gave the word *glory* a meaning for me. I still do not know where else I could have found one. I do not see how the 'fear' of God could have ever meant to me anything but the lowest prudential efforts to be safe, if I had never seen certain ominous ravines and unapproachable crags.

Ibid.

Say your prayers in a garden early, ignoring steadfastly the dew, the birds and the flowers, and you will come away overwhelmed by its freshness and joy; go there in order to be overwhelmed and, after a certain age, nine times out of ten nothing will happen to you.

Ibid.

We may find it difficult to formulate a human right of tormenting beasts in terms which would not equally imply an angelic right for tormenting men. And we may feel that though objective superiority is rightly claimed for man, yet that very superiority ought partly to *consist in* not behaving like a vivisector—that we ought to prove ourselves better than the beasts precisely by the fact of acknowledging duties to them which they do not acknowledge to us.

Vivisection

Once the old Christian idea of a total difference in kind between man and beast has been abandoned, then no argument for experiments on animals can be found which is not also an argument for experiments on inferior men. If we cut up beasts because they cannot prevent us and because we are backing our own side in the struggle for existence, it is only logical to cut up imbeciles, criminals, enemies, or capitalists for the same reason. Indeed, experiments on men have already begun.

Ibid.

Man with dog closes a gap in the universe.

The Four Loves, ch. 3

Nature has that in her which compels us to invent giants.

'On Stories', *Of Other Worlds*

[St Athanasius's] approach to the Miracles is badly needed to-day, for it is the final answer to those who object to them as 'arbitrary and meaningless violations of the laws of Nature'. They are here shown to be rather the re-telling in capital letters of the same message which Nature writes in her crabbed cursive hand; the very operations one would expect of Him who was so full of life that when He wished to die He had to 'borrow death from others'.

Introduction to *The Incarnation of the Word of God*, by St Athanasius

2. NATURE AND SUPERNATURE

We can't—or I can't—hear the song of a bird simply as a sound. Its meaning or message ('That's a bird') comes with it inevitably—just as one can't see a familiar word in print as a merely visual pattern. The reading is as involuntary as the seeing. When the wind roars I don't just hear the roar; I 'hear the wind'. In the same way it is possible to 'read' as well as to 'have' a pleasure. Or not even 'as well as'. The distinction ought to become, and sometimes is, impossible; to receive it and to recognise its divine source are a single experience. This heavenly fruit is instantly redolent of the orchard where it grew. This sweet air whispers of the country from whence it blows. It is a message. We know we are being touched by a finger of that right hand at which there are pleasures for evermore. There need be no question of thanks or praise as a separate event, something done afterwards, To experience the tiny theophany is itself to adore.

Letters to Malcolm, ch. 17

Any patch of sunlight in a wood will show you something about the sun which you could never get from reading books on astronomy. These pure and spontaneous pleasures are 'patches of Godlight' in the woods of our experience.

Ibid.

But only the strange power
Of unsought Beauty in some casual hour

Can build a bridge of light or sound or form
To lead you out of all this strife and storm. . . .
        One moment was enough,
We know we are not made of mortal stuff.
And we can bear all trials that come after,
The hate of men and the fool's loud bestial laughter
And Nature's rule and cruelties unclean,
For we have seen the Glory—we have seen.
                    'Dungeon Grates', *Spirits in Bondage*

The Naturalist thinks that the pond (Nature—the great event in space and time) is of an infinite depth—that there is nothing but water however far you go down. My claim is that some of the things on the surface (i.e. in our experience) show the contrary. These things (rational minds) reveal, on inspection, that they at least are not floating but attached by stalks to the bottom. Therefore the pond has a bottom. It is not pond, pond forever. Go deep enough and you will come to something that is not pond—to mud and earth and then to rock and finally the whole bulk of Earth and the subterranean fire.

                                        Miracles, ch. 4

The Naturalists have been engaged in thinking about Nature. They have not attended to the fact that they were *thinking*. The moment one attends to this it is obvious that one's own thinking cannot be merely a natural event, and that therefore something other than Nature exists. The Supernatural is not remote and abstruse: it is a matter of daily and hourly experience, as intimate as breathing.

                                        Ibid., ch. 6

The Naturalist believes that a great process, or 'becoming', exists 'on its own' in space and time, and that nothing else exists—what we call particular things and events being only the parts into which we analyse the great process or the shapes which that process takes at given moments and given points in space. This single, total reality he calls Nature. The Supernaturalist believes that one Thing exists on its own and has produced the framework of space and time and the procession of systematically connected events which fill them. This framework, and this filling, he calls Nature. It may, or may not, be the only reality which the one Primary Thing has produced.

Ibid., ch. 2

The various and complex conditions under which Reason and Morality appear are the twists and turns of the frontier between Nature and Supernature. That is why, if you wish, you can always ignore Supernature and treat the phenomena purely from the Natural side; just as a man studying on a map the boundaries of Cornwall and Devonshire can always say, 'What you call a bulge in Devonshire is really a dent in Cornwall'. And in a sense you can't refute him. What we call a bulge in Devonshire always *is* a dent in Cornwall. What we call rational thought in a man always involves a state of the brain, in the long run a relation of atoms. But Devonshire is none the less something more than 'where Cornwall ends', and Reason is something more than cerebral bio-chemistry.

Ibid., ch. 6

On any view, the first beginning must have been outside the ordinary process of nature. An egg which came from no bird is no more 'natural' than a bird which had existed from all eternity. And since the egg-bird-egg sequence leads us to no plausible beginning, is it not reasonable to look for the real origin somewhere outside sequence altogether?

'Who Was Right—Dream Lecturer or Real Lecturer?'
The Coventry Evening Telegraph (21 February 1945)

Only Supernaturalists really see Nature. . . . To treat her as

God, or as Everything, is to lose the whole pith and pleasure of her. Come out, look back, and then you will see ... this astonishing cataract of bears, babies, and bananas: this immoderate deluge of atoms, orchids, oranges, cancers, canaries, fleas, gases, tornadoes and toads. How could you ever have thought this was the ultimate reality? How could you ever have thought that it was merely a stage-set for the moral drama of men and women? She is herself. Offer her neither worship nor contempt. Meet her and know her. If we are immortal, and if she is doomed (as the scientists tell us) to run down and die, we shall miss this half-shy and half-flamboyant creature, this ogress, this hoyden, this incorrigible fairy, this dumb witch. But the theologians tell us that she, like ourselves, is to be redeemed. The 'vanity' to which she was subjected was her disease, not her essence. She will be cured, but cured in character: not tamed (Heaven forbid) nor sterilised. We shall still be able to recognise our old enemy, friend, playfellow and foster-mother, so perfected as to be not less, but more, herself. And that will be a merry meeting.

Miracles, ch. 9

I think every *natural* thing which is not in itself sinful can become the servant of the spiritual life, but none is automatically so.

Letters (*c*. March 1956)

We understand pictures only because we know and inhabit the three-dimensional world. If we can imagine a creature who perceived only two dimensions and yet could somehow be aware of the lines as he crawled over them on the paper, we shall easily see how impossible it would be for him to understand. At first he might be prepared to accept on authority our assurance that there was a world in three dimensions. But when we pointed to the lines on the paper and tried to explain, say, that 'This is a road', would he not reply that the shape which we were asking him to accept as a revelation of our mysterious other world was the very same shape which, on our own showing, elsewhere meant nothing but a triangle? And soon, I think, he would say, 'You keep on telling me of this other world and its unimaginable shapes which you call solid. But isn't it very suspicious that all the shapes which you offer me as images or reflections of the solid ones turn out on inspection to be simply the old two-dimensional shapes of my own world as I have always known it? Is it not obvious that your vaunted other world, so far from being the archetype, is a dream which borrows all its elements from this one?' . .

Our problem was that in what claims to be our spiritual life all the elements of our natural life recur: and, what is worse, it looks at first glance as if no other elements were present. We now see that if the spiritual is richer than the natural (as no one who believes in its existence would deny) then this is exactly what we should expect. And the sceptic's conclusion that the so-called spiritual is really derived from the natural, that it is a mirage or projection or imaginary extension of the natural, is also exactly what we should expect; for, as we have seen, this is the mistake which an observer who knew only the lower medium would be bound to make in every case of Transposition. The brutal man never can by analysis find anything but lust in love; the Flatlander never can find anything but flat shapes in a picture; physiology never can find anything in thought except twitchings of the grey matter. . . .

I am not saying that the natural act of eating after millions of years somehow blossoms into the Christian sacrament. I am saying that the Spiritual Reality, which existed before there were any creatures who ate, gives this natural act a new meaning, and more than a new meaning: makes it in a certain context to be a different thing. In a word, I think that real landscapes enter into pictures, not that pictures will one day sprout into real trees and grass.

Transposition and Other Addresses, ch. 1

Our real journey to God involves constantly turning our backs on [nature]; passing from the dawn-lit fields into some poky little church, or (it might be) going to work in an East End parish. But the love of her has been a valuable and, for some people, an indispensable initiation.

The Four Loves, ch. 2

3. GOD AS CREATOR OF NATURE

It was a Lion. Huge, shaggy, and bright it stood facing the risen sun. Its mouth was wide open in song and it was about three hundred yards away. . . . And as he walked and sang the valley grew green with grass. It spread out from the Lion like a pool. It ran up the sides of the little hills like a wave. . . . Soon there were other things besides grass. The slopes grew dark with heather. . . . And when he burst into a rapid series of lighter notes she was not surprised to see primroses suddenly appearing in every direction. . . . But now the song had once more changed. It was more like what we should call a tune, but it was also far wilder. It made you want to run and jump and climb . . . Showers of birds came out of the trees. Butterflies fluttered. Bees got to work on the flowers as if they hadn't a second to lose. . . . And now you could hardly hear the song of the Lion; there was so much cawing, cooing, crowing, braying, neighing, baying, barking, lowing, bleating, and trumpeting. . . . Then there came a swift flash like fire (but it burnt nobody) either from the sky or from the Lion itself, and every drop of blood tingled in the children's bodies, and the deepest, wildest voice they had ever heard was saying:

'Narnia, Narnia, Narnia, awake. Love. Think. Speak. Be walking trees. Be talking beasts. Be divine waters'.

The Magician's Nephew, chs. 8, 9

To say that God has created her is not to say that she is un-real, but precisely that she is real. Would you make God less creative than Shakespeare or Dickens? What He creates is created in the round: it is far more concrete than Falstaff or Sam Weller. . . . God's creative freedom is to be conceived as the freedom of a poet: the freedom to create a consistent, positive thing with its own inimitable flavour. . . . It would be a miserable error to suppose that the dimensions of space and time, the death and re-birth of vegetation, the unity in multiplicity of organisms, the union in opposition of sexes, and the colour of each particular apple in Herefordshire this autumn, were merely a collection of useful devices forcibly welded together. They are the very idiom, almost the facial expression, the smell or taste, of an individual thing. The *quality* of Nature is present in them all just as the Latinity of Latin is present in every inflection or the 'Correggiosity' of Correggio in every stroke of the brush.

Miracles, ch. 9

At the very least, there must always remain the utterly 'brute' fact, the completely opaque *datum*, that a universe—or, rather, *this* universe with its determinate character—exists; as 'magical' as the magic flower in the fairy-tale. . . .

One cannot conceive a more completely 'given', or, if you like, a more 'magical', fact than the existence of God as *causa sui*.

Letters to Malcolm, ch. 19

There is no good trying to be more spiritual than God. God never meant man to be a purely spiritual creature. That is why He uses material things like bread and wine to put the new life into us. We may think this rather crude and unspiritual. God does not: He invented eating. He likes matter. He invented it.

Mere Christianity, bk 2, ch. 5

I know some muddle-headed Christians have talked as if Christianity thought that sex, or the body, or pleasure, were bad in themselves. But they were wrong. Christianity is almost the only one of the great religions which thoroughly approves of the body—which believes that matter is good, that God Himself once took on a human body, that some kind of body is going to be given to us even in Heaven and is going to be an essential part of our happiness, our beauty, and our energy. Christianity has glorified marriage more than any other religion: and nearly all the greatest love poetry in the world has been produced by Christians.

Ibid., bk 3, ch. 5

Where a God who is totally purposive and totally foreseeing acts upon a Nature which is totally interlocked, there can be no accidents or loose ends, nothing whatever of which we can safely use the word *merely*. Nothing is 'merely a bye-product' of anything else. All results are intended from the first. What is subservient from one point of view is the main purpose from another. No thing or event is first or highest in a sense which forbids it to be also last and lowest. The partner who bows to Man in one movement of the dance receives Man's reverences in another. To be high or central means to abdicate continually: to be low means to be raised: all good masters are servants: God washes the feet of men.

Miracles, ch. 14

The objects around me, and my idea of 'me', will deceive if taken at their face value. But they are momentous if taken as the end-products of divine activities. Thus and not otherwise, the creation of matter and the creation of mind meet one another and the circuit is closed. . . .

If you start investigating the nature of matter, you will not find anything like what imagination has always supposed matter to be. You will get mathematics. From that unimaginable physical reality my senses select a few stimuli. These they translate or symbolise into sensations, which have no likeness at all to the reality of matter. Of these sensations my associative power, very much directed by my practical needs and influenced by social training, makes up little bundles into what I call 'things' (labelled by nouns). Out of these I build myself a neat little box stage, suitably provided with properties such as hills, fields, houses, and the rest. In this I can act.

Letters to Malcolm, ch. 15

It is well to have specifically holy places, and things, and days, for, without these focal points or reminders, the belief that all is holy and 'big with God' will soon dwindle into a mere senti-ment. But if these holy places, things, and days cease to remind us, if they obliterate our awareness that all ground is holy and every bush (could we but perceive it) a Burning Bush, then the hallows begin to do harm. Hence both the necessity, and the perennial danger, of 'religion'.

Ibid., ch. 14

4. NATURE, MYTH AND ALLEGORY

Death and Re-birth—go down to go up—it is a key prin-ciple. Through this bottleneck, this belittlement, the highroad nearly always lies. . . .

The pattern is there in Nature because it was first there in God. . . . The total pattern . . . is the real Death and Re-birth: for certainly no seed ever fell from so fair a tree into so dark and cold a soil as would furnish more than a faint analogy to this huge descent and re-ascension in which God dredged the salt and oozy bottom of Creation. . . .

The Corn-King is derived (through human imagination) from the facts of Nature, and the facts of Nature from her Creator; the Death and Re-birth pattern is in her because it was first in Him. On the other hand, elements of Nature-religion are strikingly absent from the teaching of Jesus and from the

Judaic preparation which led up to it precisely because in them Nature's Original is manifesting Itself.

Miracles, ch. 14

God sent the human race what I call good dreams: I mean those queer stories scattered all through the heathen religions about a god who dies and comes to life again, and by his death, has somehow given new life to men.

Mere Christianity, bk 2, ch. 3

A great myth is relevant as long as the predicament of humanity lasts: as long as humanity lasts. It will always work, on those who can receive it, the same catharsis. . . .

It deals with the permanent and inevitable, whereas . . . a ten mile walk or even a dose of salts might annihilate many of the problems in which the characters of a refined and subtle novel are entangled.

'Haggard Rides Again', *Time and Tide*
(3 September 1960)

The Divine light, we are told, 'lighteneth every man'. We should, therefore, expect to find in the imagination of great Pagan teachers and myth-makers some glimpse of that theme which we believe to be the very plot of the whole cosmic story—the theme of incarnation, death and re-birth. And the differences between the Pagan Christs (Balder, Osiris, etc.) and the Christ Himself is much what we should expect to find. The Pagan stories are all about someone dying and rising, either every year, or else nobody knows where and nobody knows when. The Christian story is about a historical personage, whose execution can be dated pretty accurately, under a named Roman magistrate, and with whom the society that He founded is in a continuous relation down to the present day. It is not the difference between falsehood and truth. It is the

difference between a real event on the one hand and dim
dreams or premonitions of that same event on the other.

They Asked for a Paper, ch. 9

But then another voice spoke to him from behind him,
saying:

'Child, if you will, it *is* mythology. It is but truth, not fact:
an image, not the very real. But then it is My mythology. The
words of Wisdom are also myth and metaphor: but since they
do not know themselves for what they are, in them the hidden
myth is master, where it should be servant: and it is but of
man's inventing. But this is My inventing, this is the veil under
which I have chosen to appear even from the first until now.
For this end I made your senses and for this end your imagination, that you might see my face and live.'

The Pilgrim's Regress, bk 9, ch. 5

As myth transcends thought, Incarnation transcends myth.
The heart of Christianity is a myth which is also a fact. The old
myth of the Dying God, *without ceasing to be myth*, comes down
from the heaven of legend and imagination to the earth of history. It *happens*—at a particular date, in a particular place, followed
by definable historical consequences. We pass from a Balder or
an Osiris, dying nobody knows when or where, to a historical
Person crucified (it is all in order) *under Pontius Pilate*. By
becoming fact it does not cease to be myth: that is the miracle.
I suspect that men have sometimes derived more spiritual
sustenance from myths they did not believe than from the
religion they professed. To be truly Christian we must both
assent to the historical fact and also receive the myth (fact
though it has become) with the same imaginative embrace
which we accord to all myths. The one is hardly more necessary than the other.... We must not be ashamed of the
mythical radiance resting on our theology.

'Myth Became Fact', *World Dominion*
(September–October 1944)

The belief that Myth in general is not merely misunderstood history (as Euhemerus thought) nor diabolical illusion (as some of the Fathers thought) nor priestly lying (as the philosophers of the Enlightenment thought) but, at its best, a real though un-focussed gleam of divine truth falling on human imagination.

Miracles, ch. 15

If Christianity is only a mythology, then I find the myth-ology I believe in is not the one I like best. I like Greek myth-ology much better: Irish better still: Norse best of all.

They Asked for a Paper, ch. 9

Ransom had been perceiving that the triple distinction of truth from myth and of both from fact was purely terrestrial—was part and parcel of that unhappy division between soul and body which resulted from the Fall. Even on earth the sacra-ments existed as a permanent reminder that the division was neither wholesome nor final. The Incarnation had been the beginning of its disappearance.

Perelandra, ch. 11

Mr Bultitude's mind was as furry and as unhuman in shape as his body. . . . He did not know that they were people, nor that he was a bear. Indeed, he did not know that he existed at all: everything that is represented by the words *I* and *Me* and *Thou* was absent from his mind. When Mrs Maggs gave him a tin of golden syrup, as she did every Sunday morning, he did not recognise either a giver or a recipient. Goodness occurred and he tasted it. And that was all. . . . There was no prose in his life. The appetencies which a human mind might disdain as cup-board loves were for him quivering and ecstatic aspirations which absorbed his whole being, infinite yearnings, stabbed with the threat of tragedy and shot through with the colours of Paradise. One of our race, if plunged back for a moment in the

warm, trembling, iridescent pool of that pre-Adamite consciousness, would have emerged believing that he had grasped
the absolute; for the states below reason and the states above it
have, by their common contrast to the life we know, a certain
superficial resemblance. Sometimes there returns to us from
infancy the memory of a nameless delight or terror, unattached
to any delightful or dreadful thing, 'a potent adjective floating
in a nounless void, a pure quality'. At such moments we have
experience of the shallows of that pool. But fathoms deeper
than any memory can take us, right down in the central
warmth and dimness, the bear lived all its life.

That Hideous Strength, ch. 14

Myth is thus like manna; it is to each man a different dish and
to each the dish he needs. It does not grow old nor stick at
frontiers racial, sexual, or philosophic; and even from the same
man at the same moment it can elicit different responses at
different levels. But great myth is rare in a reflective age; the
temptation to allegorize, to thrust into the story the conscious
doctrines of the poet, there to fight it out as best they can with
the inherent tendency of the fable, is usually too strong.

Rehabilitations, ch. 1

All my deepest, and certainly all my earliest, experiences
seem to be of sheer quality. The terrible and the lovely are
older and solider than terrible and lovely things. If a musical
phrase could be translated into words at all it would become an
adjective. A great lyric is very like a long, utterly adequate,
adjective. Plato was not so silly as the Moderns think when he
elevated abstract nouns—that is, adjectives disguised as nouns—
into the supreme realities—the Forms.

Letters to Malcolm, ch. 16

It is of the very nature of thought and language to represent
what is immaterial in pictureable terms. What is good or happy

has always been high like the heavens and bright like the sun. Evil and misery were deep and dark from the first. . . . To ask how these married pairs of sensibles and insensibles first came together would be great folly; the real question is how they ever came apart. . . .

But there is another way of using the equivalence, which is almost the opposite of allegory, and which I would call sacramentalism or symbolism. If our passions, being immaterial, can be copied by material inventions, then it is possible that our material world in its turn is the copy of an invisible world. As the god Amor and his figurative garden are to the actual passions of men, so perhaps we ourselves and our 'real' world are to something else. The attempt to read that something else through its sensible imitations, to see the archtype in the copy, is what I mean by symbolism or sacramentalism. It is, in fine, 'the philosophy of Hermes that this visible world is but a picture of the invisible, wherein, as in a portrait, things are not truly but in equivocal shapes, as they counterfeit some real substance in that invisible fabrick'. The difference between the two can hardly be exaggerated. The allegorist leaves the given—his own passions—to talk of that which is confessedly less real, which is a fiction. The symbolist leaves the given to find that which is more real. To put the difference in another way, for the symbolist it is we who are the allegory.

The Allegory of Love, ch. 2, sec. 1

[We have] in Gower's *Confessio Amantis* one of those rare passages in which medieval allegory rises to myth, in which the symbols, though fashioned to represent mere single concepts, take on new life and represent rather the principles—not otherwise accessible—which unite whole classes of concepts. All is shot through with meanings which the author may never have been aware of; and, on this level, it does not matter whether he was or not. . . . Doubtless it is a rule in poetry that if you do

your own work well, you will find you have done also work
you never dreamed of.

Ibid., ch. 5, sec. 1

It is a mischievous error to suppose that in an allegory the
author is 'really' talking about the thing symbolized, and not at
all about the thing that symbolizes; the very essence of the art is
to talk about both.

Ibid., ch. 5, sec. 2

Some readers cannot enjoy . . . shepherds because they know
(or they say they know) that real country people are not more
happy or more virtuous than anyone else; but it would be
tedious . . . to explain to them the many causes (reasons too)
that have led humanity to symbolize by rural scenes and
occupations a region in the mind which does exist and which
should be visited often. If they know the region, let them try
to people it with tram conductors or policemen, and I shall
applaud any success they may have; if not, who can help them?

Ibid., ch. 7, sec. 3

X

THE POST-CHRISTIAN WORLD

1. THE MODERN VIEW

Between Jane Austen and us comes the birth of the machines.
... This is parallel to the great changes by which we divide
epochs of pre-history. This is on a level with the change from
stone to bronze, or from a pastoral to an agricultural economy.
It alters Man's place in nature. . . .

I conclude that it really is the greatest change in the history of
Western Man.

They Asked for a Paper, ch. 1

'It is the same with all their machines. Their labour-saving
devices multiply drudgery; their aphrodisiacs make them im-
potent; their amusements bore them; their rapid production of
food leaves half of them starving, and their devices for saving
time have banished leisure from their country.'

The Pilgrim's Regress, bk 10, ch. 6

At the outset, the universe appears packed with will, intelligence, life and positive qualities; every tree is a nymph and
every planet a god. Man himself is akin to the gods. The
advance of knowledge gradually empties this rich and genial
universe: first of its gods, then of its colours, smells, sounds and
tastes, finally of solidity itself as solidity was originally imagined. As these items are taken from the world, they are trans-
ferred to the subjective side of the account: classified as our

sensations, thoughts, images or emotions. The Subject becomes gorged, inflated, at the expense of the Object. But the matter does not end there. The same method which has emptied the world now proceeds to empty ourselves. The masters of the method soon announce that we were just as mistaken (and mistaken in much the same way) when we attributed 'souls', or 'selves' or 'minds' to human organisms, as when we attributed Dryads to the trees. . . . We, who have personified all other things, turn out to be ourselves mere personifications. . . . And thus we arrived at a result uncommonly like zero. While we were reducing the world to almost nothing we deceived ourselves with the fancy that all its lost qualities were being kept safe (if in a somewhat humbled condition) as 'things in our own mind'. Apparently we had no mind of the sort required. The Subject is as empty as the Object. Almost nobody has been making linguistic mistakes about almost nothing. By and large, this is the only thing that has ever happened.

Preface to D. E. Harding's
Hierarchy of Heaven and Earth

. . . a whole nation of eyeless men,
Dark bipeds not aware how they were maimed.

'The Country of the Blind,' *Poems*

How has it come about that we use the highly emotive word 'stagnation', with all its malodorous and malarial overtones, for what other ages would have called 'permanence'? Why does the word 'primitive' at once suggest to us clumsiness, inefficiency, barbarity? . . . Why does 'latest' in advertisements mean 'best'? . . . I submit that what has imposed this climate of opinion so firmly on the human mind is a new archetypal image. It is the image of old machines being superseded by new and better ones. For in the world of machines the new most often really is better and the primitive really is the clumsy. And this image, potent in all our minds, reigns almost without rival in the minds of the uneducated. For to them, after their marriage and the births of their children, the very milestones of life are technical advances.

They Asked for a Paper, ch. 1

A man is likely to become 'dated' . . . precisely because he is anxious not to be dated, to be 'contemporary': for to move with the times is, of course, to go where all times go.

'Period Criticism', *Time and Tide*
(9 November 1946)

I was in that state of mind in which a boy thinks it extremely telling to call God *Jahveh* and Jesus *Yeshua*.

Surprised by Joy, ch. 11

It took me as long to acquire inhibitions as others (they say) have taken to get rid of them. That is why I often find myself at such cross-purposes with the modern world: I have been a converted Pagan living among apostate Puritans.

Ibid., ch. 4

We must get rid of our arrogant assumption that it is the masses who can be led by the nose. As far as I can make out, the shoe is on the other foot. The only people who are really the dupes of their favourite newspapers are the *intelligentsia*.

'Private Bates', *The Spectator*
(29 December 1944)

The whole modern estimate of primitive man is based upon that idolatry of artefacts which is a great corporate sin of our own civilisation. We forget that our prehistoric ancestors made all the most useful discoveries, except that of chloroform, which have ever been made. To them we owe language, the family, clothing, the use of fire, the domestication of animals, the wheel, the ship, poetry and agriculture.

The Problem of Pain, ch. 5

The modern who dislikes the Christian Fathers would have disliked the Pagan philosophers equally, and for similar reasons. Both alike would have embarrassed him with stories of visions, ecstasies, and apparitions.

The Discarded Image, ch. 4

[Owen Barfield] made short work of what I have called my 'chronological snobbery', the uncritical acceptance of the intellectual climate common to our own age and the assumption that whatever has gone out of date is on that account discredited. You must find why it went out of date. Was it ever refuted (and if so by whom, where, and how conclusively) or did it merely die away as fashions do? If the latter, this tells us nothing about its truth or falsehood. From seeing this, one passes to the realisation that our own age is also 'a period', and certainly has, like all periods, its own characteristic illusions. They are likeliest to lurk in those wide-spread assumptions which are so ingrained in the age that no one dares to attack or feels it necessary to defend them.

Surprised by Joy, ch. 13

You will hear people say, 'The early Christians believed that Christ was the son of a virgin, but we know that this is a scientific impossibility.' Such people seem to have an idea that belief in miracles arose at a period when men were so ignorant of the course of nature that they did not perceive a miracle to be contrary to it. A moment's thought shows this to be nonsense: and the story of the Virgin Birth is a particularly striking example. When St. Joseph discovered that his fiancée was going to have a baby, he not unnaturally decided to repudiate her. Why? Because he knew just as well as any modern gynaecologist that in the ordinary course of nature women do not have babies unless they have lain with men. . . . In any sense in which it is true to say now, 'The thing is scientifically impossible,' he would have said the same. . . . Belief in miracles, far from depending on an ignorance of the laws of nature, is only possible in so far as those laws are known.

Miracles, ch. 7

There can be no moral motive for entering a new morality unless that motive is borrowed from the traditional morality. ... All the specifically modern attempts at new moralities are contradictions. They proceed by retaining some traditional precepts and rejecting others: but the only real authority behind those which they retain is the very same authority which they flout in rejecting others. ... You can attack the concept of justice because it interferes with the feeding of the masses, but you have taken the duty of feeding the masses from the world-wide code. You may exalt patriotism at the expense of mercy; but it was the old code that told you to love your country. You may vivisect your grandfather in order to deliver your grandchildren from cancer: but, take away traditional morality, and why should you bother about your grandchildren?

'On Ethics', *Christian Reflections*

That elementary rectitude of human response, at which we are so ready to fling the unkind epithets of 'stock', 'crude', 'bourgeois', and 'conventional', so far from being 'given' is a delicate balance of trained habits, laboriously acquired and easily lost, on the maintenance of which depend both our virtues and our pleasures and even, perhaps, the survival of our species. For though the human heart is not unchanging (nay changes almost out of recognition in the twinkling of an eye) the laws of causation are. When poisons become fashionable they do not cease to kill. ...

The older poetry, by continually insisting on certain Stock themes—as that love is sweet, death bitter, virtue lovely, and children or gardens delightful—was performing a service not only of moral and civil, but even of biological, importance.

A Preface to 'Paradise Lost', ch. 8

To study the past does indeed liberate us from the present, from the idols of our own market-place. But I think it liberates us from the past too. I think no class of men are less enslaved to the past than historians. The unhistorical are usually, without knowing it, enslaved to a fairly recent past.

They Asked for a Paper, ch. 1

Christians and Pagans had much more in common with each other than either has with a post-Christian. The gap between those who worship different gods is not so wide as that between those who worship and those who do not. . . .

A post-Christian man is not a Pagan; you might as well think that a married woman recovers her virginity by divorce. The post-Christian is cut off from the Christian past and therefore doubly from the Pagan past.

Ibid.

A society where the simple many obey the few seers can live: a society where all were seers could live even more fully. But a society where the mass is still simple and the seers are no longer attended to can achieve only superficiality, baseness, ugliness, and in the end extinction. On or back we must go; to stay here is death.

Miracles, ch. 6

There was a boy called Eustace Clarence Scrubb, and he almost deserved it. His parents called him Eustace Clarence and his school-masters called him Scrubb. I can't tell you how his friends spoke to him, for he had none. He didn't call his father and mother 'Father' and 'Mother', but Harold and Alberta. They were very up-to-date and advanced people. They were vegetarians, non-smokers and teetotallers and wore a special kind of underclothes. In their house there was very little furniture and very few clothes on the beds, and the windows were always open.

Eustace Clarence liked animals, especially beetles, if they were dead and pinned on a card. He liked books if they were books of information and had pictures of grain elevators or of fat foreign children doing exercises in model schools.

The Voyage of the 'Dawn Treader', ch. 1

The ancient man approached God (or even the gods) as the accused person approaches his judge. For the modern man the *rôles* are reversed. He is the judge: God is in the dock. He is quite a kindly judge: if God should have a reasonable defence for being the god who permits war, poverty and disease, he is ready to listen to it. The trial may even end in God's acquittal. But the important thing is that Man is on the Bench and God in the Dock.

'Difficulties in Presenting the Christian Faith to Modern Unbelievers', *Lumen Vitae* (September 1948)

The knight is a man of blood and iron, a man familiar with the sight of smashed faces and the ragged stumps of lopped-off limbs; he is also a demure, almost a maidenlike, guest in hall, a gentle, modest, unobtrusive man. He is not a compromise or happy mean between ferocity and meekness; he is fierce to the *n*th and meek to the *n*th. . . .

Will the *ethos* [of a classless society] be a synthesis of what was best in all the classes or a mere 'pool' with the sediment of all and the virtues of none?

'Notes on the Way', *Time and Tide* (17 August 1940)

There is a crowd of busybodies, self-appointed masters of ceremonies, whose life is devoted to destroying solitude wherever solitude still exists. . . . If an Augustine, a Vaughan, a Traherne or a Wordsworth should be born in the modern world, the leaders of a Youth Organization would soon cure him. . . . We live, in fact, in a world starved for solitude, silence, and privacy: and therefore starved for meditation and true friendship.

Transposition and Other Addresses, ch. 3

Nowadays it seems to be so forgotten that people think they have somehow discredited Our Lord if they can show that some pre-Christian document (or what they take to be pre-Christian) such as the Dead Sea Scrolls has 'anticipated' Him. As if we supposed Him to be a cheapjack like Nietzsche inventing a new ethics! Every good teacher, within Judaism as without, has anticipated Him. The whole religious history of the pre-Christian world, on its better side, anticipates Him. It could not be otherwise. The Light which has lightened every man from the beginning may shine more clearly but cannot change. The Origin cannot suddenly start being, in the popular sense of the word, 'original'.

Reflections on the Psalms, ch. 3

Christians and their opponents again and again expect that some new discovery will either turn matters of faith into matters of knowledge or else reduce them to patent absurdities. But it has never happened.

The World's Last Night, ch. 6

'In our world', said Eustace, 'a star is a huge ball of flaming gas.'

'Even in your world, my son, that is not what a star is but only what it is made of.'

The Voyage of the 'Dawn Treader', ch. 14

Atoms dead could never thus
Stir the human heart of us
Unless the beauty that we see
The veil of endless beauty be,
Filled full of spirits that have trod

Far hence along the heavenly sod
And seen the bright footprints of God.
                          'Song', *Spirits in Bondage*

Mere is always a dangerous word.
                          The Four Loves, ch. 1

The strength of such a [naturalistic] critic lies in the words 'merely' or 'nothing but'. He sees all the facts but not the meaning. Quite truly, therefore, he claims to have seen all the facts. There *is* nothing else there; except the meaning. He is therefore, as regards the matter in hand, in the position of an animal. You will have noticed that most dogs cannot understand *pointing*. You point to a bit of food on the floor: the dog, instead of looking at the floor, sniffs at your finger. A finger is a finger to him, and that is all. His world is all fact and no meaning. And in a period when factual realism is dominant we shall find people deliberately inducing upon themselves this doglike mind. A man who has experienced love from within will deliberately go about to inspect it analytically from outside and regard the results of this analysis as truer than his experience. The extreme limit of this self-blinding is seen in those who, like the rest of us, have consciousness, yet go about to study the human organism as if they did not know it was conscious. As long as this deliberate refusal to understand things from above, even where such understanding is possible, continues, it is idle to talk of any final victory over materialism. The critique of every experience from below, the voluntary ignoring of meaning and concentration on fact, will always have the same plausibility. There will always be evidence, and every month fresh evidence, to show that religion is only psychological, justice only self-protection, politics only economics, love only lust, and thought itself only cerebral biochemistry.

                          Transposition and Other Addresses, ch. 1

Determinism does not deny the existence of human behaviour. It rejects as an illusion our spontaneous conviction that our behaviour has its ultimate origin in ourselves. What I call 'my act' is the conduit-pipe through which the torrent of the universal process passes, and was bound to pass, at a particular time and place. The distinction between what we call the 'voluntary' and the 'involuntary' movements of our own bodies is not obliterated, but turns out (on this view) to be not exactly the sort of difference we supposed. What I call the 'involuntary' movements necessarily—and, if we know enough, predictably —result from mechanical causes outside my body or from pathological or organic processes within it. The 'voluntary' ones result from conscious psychological factors which themselves result from unconscious psychological factors dependent on my economic situation, my infantile and pre-natal experience, my heredity . . . and so on back to the beginnings of organic life and beyond. I am a conductor, not a source. I never make an original contribution to the world-process. I move with that process not even as a floating log moves with the river but as a particular pint of the water itself moves.

Letters to Malcolm, ch. 7

If the solar system was brought about by an accidental collision, then the appearance of organic life on this planet was also an accident, and the whole evolution of Man was an accident too. If so, then all our present thoughts are mere accidents—the accidental by-product of the movement of atoms. And this holds for the thoughts of the materialists and astronomers as well as for anyone else's. But if *their* thoughts— i.e., of Materialism and Astronomy—are merely accidental by-products, why should we believe them to be true? I see no reason for believing that one accident should be able to give me a correct account of all the other accidents. It's like expecting that the accidental shape taken by the splash when you upset a

milk-jug should give you a correct account of how the jug
was made and why it was upset.

Answers to Questions on Christianity

The theory that thought is merely a movement in the brain
is, in my opinion, nonsense; for if so, that theory itself would
be merely a movement, an event among atoms, which may
have speed and direction but of which it would be meaningless
to use the words 'true' or 'false'.

Transposition and Other Addresses, ch. 1

It is widely believed that scientific thought does put us in
touch with reality, whereas moral or metaphysical thought
does not. . . . The cycle of scientific thought is from experiment to hypothesis and thence to verification and a new hypothesis. Experiment means sense-experiences specially arranged.
Verification involves inference. 'If X existed, then, under
conditions Y, we should have the experience Z.' We then produce the conditions Y and Z appears. We thence infer the
existence of X. Now it is clear that the only part of this process
which assures us of any reality outside ourselves is precisely the
inference 'If X, then Z', or conversely 'Since Z, therefore X'.
The other parts of the process, namely hypothesis and experiment, cannot by themselves give us any assurance. The hypothesis is, admittedly, a mental construction—something, as
they say, 'inside our own heads'. And the experiment is a state
of our own consciousness. . . . The physical sciences, then,
depend on the validity of logic just as much as metaphysics or
mathematics. . . . We should therefore abandon the distinction between scientific and non-scientific thought.

'De Futilitate', Christian Reflections

Granted that Reason is prior to matter and that the light of
that primal Reason illuminates finite minds, I can understand

how men should come, by observation and inference, to know a lot about the universe they live in. If, on the other hand, I swallow the scientific cosmology as a whole, then not only can I not fit in Christianity, but I cannot even fit in science. If minds are wholly dependent on brains, and brains on bio-chemistry, and bio-chemistry (in the long run) on the meaningless flux of the atoms, I cannot understand how the thought of those minds should have any more significance than the sound of the wind in the trees . . . . The waking world is judged more real because it can thus contain the dreaming world: the dreaming world is judged less real because it cannot contain the waking one. For the same reason I am certain that in passing from the scientific point of view to the theological, I have passed from dream to waking. Christian theology can fit in science, art, morality, and the sub-Christian religions. The scientific point of view cannot fit in any of these things, not even science itself. I believe in Christianity as I believe that the Sun has risen not only because I see it but because by it I see everything else.

They Asked for a Paper, ch. 9

Mechanism, like all materialist systems, breaks down at the problem of knowledge. If thought is the undesigned and irrelevant product of cerebral motions, what reason have we to trust it? As for emergent evolution, if anyone insists on using the word *God* to mean 'whatever the universe happens to be going to do next', of course we cannot prevent him. But nobody would in fact so use it unless he had a secret belief that what is coming next will be an improvement. Such a belief, besides being unwarranted, presents peculiar difficulties to an emergent evolutionist. If things can improve, this means that there must be some absolute standard of good above and outside the cosmic process to which that process can approximate. There is no sense in talking of 'becoming better' if better means simply 'what we are becoming'—it is like congratulating yourself on reaching your destination and defining destination as 'the place you have reached'. Mellontolatry, or the worship of the future, is a *fuddled* religion.

'Evil and God', *The Spectator* (7 February 1941)

You cannot go on 'explaining away' for ever: you will find that you have explained explanation itself away. You cannot go on 'seeing through' things for ever. The whole point of seeing through something is to see something through it. It is good that the window should be transparent, because the street or garden beyond it is opaque. How if you saw through the garden too? It is no use trying to 'see through' first principles. If you see through everything, then everything is transparent. But a wholly transparent world is an invisible world. To 'see through' all things is the same as not to see.

The Abolition of Man, ch. 3

In so far as [Psychoanalysis] attempts to *heal*, i.e. to make better, every treatment involves a value-judgement. This could be avoided if the analyst said, 'Tell me what sort of a chap you want to be and I'll see how near that I can make you'; but of course he really has his own idea of what goodness and happiness consist in and works to that. And his idea is derived, not from his science (it couldn't) but from his age, sex, class, culture, religion and heredity, and is just as much in need of criticism as the patient's.

Letters (26 March 1940)

A great many of those who 'debunk' traditional or (as they would say) 'sentimental' values have in the background values of their own which they believe to be immune from the debunking process.

The Abolition of Man, ch. 2

The Existentialist feels *Angst* because he thinks that man's nature (and therefore his relation to all things) has to be created or invented, without guidance, at each moment of decision. Spenser thought that man's nature was given, discoverable, and discovered; he did not feel *Angst*. He was often sad: but not, at bottom, worried.

English Literature in the Sixteenth Century, bk 3, ch. 1

To the Materialist things like nations, classes, civilizations must be more important than individuals, because the individuals live only seventy odd years each and the group may last for centuries. But to the Christian, individuals are more important, for they live eternally; and races, civilizations and the like, are in comparison the creatures of a day.

Man or Rabbit?

The Christian and the Materialist hold different beliefs about the universe. They can't both be right. The one who is wrong will act in a way which simply doesn't fit the real universe. Consequently, with the best will in the world, he will be helping his fellow creatures to their destruction.

Ibid.

The general rule which we have now pretty well established among them is that in all experiences which can make them happier or better only the physical facts are 'Real' while the spiritual elements are 'subjective'. . . . Your patient, properly handled, will have no difficulty in regarding his emotion at the sight of human entrails as a revelation of Reality and his emotion at the sight of happy children or fair weather as mere sentiment.

The Screwtape Letters, ch. 30

In vain did Ransom try to remember that he had been in 'space' and found it Heaven, tingling with a fulness of life for which infinity itself was not one cubic inch too large. All that seemed like a dream. That opposite mode of thought which he had often mocked and called in mockery, The Empirical Bogey, came surging into his mind—the great myth of our century with its gases and galaxies, its light years and evolutions, its nightmare perspectives of simple arithmetic in which everything that can possibly hold significance for the mind becomes the mere by-product of essential disorder.

Perelandra, ch. 13

Monarchy can easily be 'debunked'; but watch the faces, mark well the accents, of the debunkers. These are the men whose tap-root in Eden has been cut: whom no rumour of the polyphony, the dance, can reach—men to whom pebbles laid in a row are more beautiful than an arch. Yet even if they desire mere equality they cannot reach it. Where men are forbidden to honour a king they honour millionaires, athletes, or film-stars instead; even famous prostitutes or gangsters. For spiritual nature, like bodily nature, will be served; deny it food and it will gobble poison.

'Equality', *The Spectator* (27 August 1943)

The truest and most horrible claim made for modern transport is that it 'annihilates space'. It does. It annihilates one of the most glorious gifts we have been given. It is a vile inflation which lowers the value of distance, so that a modern boy travels a hundred miles with less sense of liberation and pilgrimage and adventure than his grandfather got from travelling ten. Of course if a man hates space and wants it to be annihilated, that is another matter. Why not creep into his coffin at once? There is little enough space there.

Surprised by Joy, ch. 10

No moonlit night will ever be the same to me again if, as I look up at that pale disc, I must think 'Yes: up there to the left is the Russian area, and over there to the right is the American bit. And up at the top is the place which is now threatening to produce a crisis.' The immemorial Moon—the Moon of the myths, the poets, the lovers—will have been taken from us forever. Part of our mind, a huge mass of our emotional wealth, will have gone. Artemis, Diana, the silver planet belonged in that fashion to all humanity: he who first reaches it steals something from us all.

'The Seeing Eye', *Christian Reflections*

2. MATERIALISM, DETERMINISM AND OBJECTIVE VALUE

Men became scientific because they expected Law in Nature, and they expected Law in Nature because they believed in a Legislator. In most modern scientists this belief has died: it will be interesting to see how long their confidence in uniformity survives it. Two significant developments have already appeared—the hypothesis of a lawless sub-nature, and the surrender of the claim that science is true. We may be living nearer than we suppose to the end of the Scientific Age.

Miracles, ch. 13

Every scientific statement in the long run, however complicated it looks, really means something like, 'I pointed the telescope to such and such a part of the sky at 2:20 A.M. on January 15th and saw so-and-so,' or, 'I put some of this stuff in a pot and heated it to such-and-such a temperature and it did so-and-so.' Do not think I am saying anything against science: I am only saying what its job is. And the more scientific a man is, the more (I believe) he would agree with me that this is the job of science—and a very useful and necessary job it is too. But why anything comes to be there at all, and whether there is anything behind the things science observes—something of a different kind—this is not a scientific question. If there is

'Something Behind', then either it will have to remain alto-gether unknown to men or else make itself known in some different way. The statement that there is any such thing, and the statement that there is no such thing, are neither of them statements that science can make. . . . Supposing science ever became complete so that it knew every single thing in the whole universe. Is it not plain that the questions, 'Why is there a universe?' 'Why does it go on as it does?' 'Has it any mean-ing?' would remain just as they were?

Mere Christianity, bk 1, ch. 4

John was silent for a few minutes. Then he began again: 'But how do you *know* there is no Landlord?'

'Christopher Columbus, Galileo, the earth is round, inven-tion of printing, gunpowder!!' exclaimed Mr. Enlightenment in such a loud voice that the pony shied.

The Pilgrim's Regress, bk 2, ch. 1

By universal evolutionism I mean the belief that the very formula of universal process is from imperfect to perfect, from small beginnings to great endings, from the rudimentary to the elaborate: the belief which makes people find it natural to think that morality springs from savage taboos, adult senti-ment from infantile sexual maladjustments, thought from instinct, mind from matter, organic from inorganic, cosmos from chaos. This is perhaps the deepest habit of mind in the contemporary world. It seems to me immensely unplausible, because it makes the general course of nature so very unlike those parts of nature we can observe.

They Asked for a Paper, ch. 9

One reason why many people find Creative Evolution so attractive is that it gives one much of the emotional comfort of believing in God and none of the less pleasant consequences. When you are feeling fit and the sun is shining and you do not want to believe that the whole universe is a mere mechanical dance of atoms, it is nice to be able to think of this great mysterious Force rolling on through the centuries and carrying you on its crest. If, on the other hand, you want to do something rather shabby, the Life-Force, being only a blind force, with no morals and no mind, will never interfere with you like that troublesome God we learned about when we were children. The Life-Force is a sort of tame God. You can switch it on when you want, but it will not bother you. All the thrills of religion and none of the cost. Is the Life-Force the greatest achievement of wishful thinking the world has yet seen?

Mere Christianity, bk 1, ch. 4

There is lodged in popular thought the conception that improvement is, somehow, a cosmic law: a conception to which the sciences give no support at all. There is no general tendency even for organisms to improve. There is no evidence that the mental and moral capacities of the human race have been increased since man became man. And there is certainly no tendency for the universe as a whole to move in any direction which we should call 'good'.

'*De Futilitate*', *Christian Reflections*

Evolution is not only not a doctrine of *moral* improvement, it is not even a doctrine of biological improvement, but of biological changes, some improvements, some deteriorations.

Letters (1 August 1949)

There is no general law of progress in biological history. . . . No one looking at world history without some preconception in favor of progress could find it in a steady up gradient. . . . The idea which here shuts out the Second Coming from our minds, the idea of the world slowly ripening to perfection, is a myth, not a generalization from experience.

The World's Last Night, ch. 7

What is vital and healthy does not necessarily survive. Higher organisms are often conquered by lower ones. . . . We ask too often why cultures perish and too seldom why they survive; as though their conservation were the normal and obvious fact and their death the abnormality for which special causes must be found. It is not so. An art, a whole civilization, may at any time slip through men's fingers in a very few years and be gone beyond recovery. If we are alive when such a thing is happening we shall hardly notice it until too late: and it is most unlikely that we shall know its causes.

English Literature in the Sixteenth Century, bk 1, ch. 1

Experience beats in vain upon a congenital progressive.

Ibid., Introduction

The demand for a developing world . . . grows up first; when it is full grown the scientists go to work and discover the evidence on which our belief in that sort of universe would now be held to rest. There is no question here of the old Model's being shattered by the inrush of new phenomena. The truth would seem to be the reverse; that when changes in the human mind produce a sufficient disrelish of the old Model and a sufficient hankering for some new one, phenomena to support that new one will obediently turn up. I do not at all mean that these new phenomena are illusory. Nature has all sorts of phenomena in stock and can suit many different tastes.

The Discarded Image, Epilogue

In modern, that is, in evolutionary, thought Man stands at the top of a stair whose foot is lost in obscurity; in [medieval thought] he stands at the bottom of a stair whose top is invisible with light.

Ibid., ch. 4, sec. C

One of the most dangerous errors instilled into us by nineteenth-century progressive optimism is the idea that civilization is automatically bound to increase and spread. The lesson of history is the opposite; civilization is a rarity, attained with difficulty and easily lost. The normal state of humanity is barbarism, just as the normal surface of our planet is salt water. . . . Human life means to me the life of beings for whom the leisured activities of thought, art, literature, conversation are the end, and the preservation and propagation of life merely the means. That is why education seems to me so important: it actualizes that potentiality for leisure, if you like for amateurishness, which is man's prerogative.

Rehabilitations, ch. 4

One thing, however, marriage has done for me. I can never again believe that religion is manufactured out of our unconscious, starved desires and is a substitute for sex. For those few years H. and I feasted on love; every mode of it—solemn and merry, romantic and realistic, sometimes as dramatic as a thunder-storm, sometimes as comfortable and unemphatic as putting on your soft slippers. No cranny of heart or body remained unsatisfied. If God were a substitute for love we ought to have lost all interest in Him. Who'd bother about substitutes when he has the thing itself? But that isn't what happens. We both knew we wanted something besides one another—quite a different kind of something, a quite different kind of want.

A Grief Observed, ch. 1

We are told to 'get things out into the open', not for the sake of self-humiliation, but on the ground that these 'things' are very natural and we need not be ashamed of them. But unless Christianity is wholly false, the perception of ourselves which we have in moments of shame must be the only true one. . . . In trying to extirpate Shame we have broken down one of the ramparts of the human spirit. . . . The 'frankness' of people sunk below shame is a very cheap frankness.

A recovery of the old sense of sin is essential to Christianity.

The Problem of Pain, ch. 4

But there is also a merely morbid and fidgety curiosity about one's self—the slop-over from modern psychology—which surely does no good? The unfinished picture would so like to jump off the easel and have a look at itself! And analysis doesn't cure that. We all know people who have undergone it and seem to have made themselves a lifelong subject of research ever since.

Letters to Malcolm, ch. 6

Keep clear of psychiatrists unless you know that they are also Christians. Otherwise they start with the assumption that your religion is an illusion and try to 'cure' it: and this assumption they make not as professional psychologists but as amateur philosophers. Often they have never given the question any serious thought.

Letters (*c*. October 1947)

The presence which we voluntarily evade is often, and we know it, His presence in wrath.

And out of this evil comes a good. If I never fled from His presence, then I should suspect those moments when I seemed to delight in it of being wish-fulfilment dreams. That, by the way, explains the feebleness of all those water versions of Christianity which leave out all the darker elements and try to establish a religion of pure consolation. No real belief in the watered versions can last. Bemused and besotted as we are, we still dimly know at heart that nothing which is at all times and in every way agreeable to us can have objective reality. It is of the very nature of the real that it should have sharp corners and rough edges, that it should be resistant, should be itself.

Dream-furniture is the only kind on which you never stub your toes or bang your knee.

Letters to Malcolm, ch. 14

Mathematicians, astronomers, and physicists are often religious, even mystical; biologists much less often; economists and psychologists very seldom indeed. It is as their subject matter comes nearer to man himself that their anti-religious bias hardens.

'Religion without Dogma', *Socratic Digest* (1948)

In our age I think it would be fair to say that the ease with which a scientific theory assumes the dignity and rigidity of fact varies inversely with the individual's scientific education.

The Discarded Image, ch. 2

In science we have been reading only the notes to a poem; in Christianity we find the poem itself.

Miracles, ch. 14

3. EDUCATION AND RELIGION

Almost our whole education has been directed to silencing this shy, persistent, inner voice; almost all our modern philosophies have been devised to convince us that the good of man is to be found on this earth. And yet it is a remarkable thing that such philosophies of Progress or Creative Evolution themselves bear reluctant witness to the truth that our real goal is elsewhere. When they want to convince you that earth is your home, notice how they set about it. They begin by trying to persuade you that earth can be made into heaven, thus giving a sop to your sense of exile in earth as it is. Next, they tell you that this fortunate event is still a good way off in the future, thus giving a sop to your knowledge that the fatherland is not here and now.

Transposition and Other Addresses, ch. 2

For every one pupil who needs to be guarded from a weak excess of sensibility there are three who need to be awakened from the slumber of cold vulgarity. The task of the modern educator is not to cut down jungles but to irrigate deserts. The right defence against false sentiments is to inculcate just sentiments. By starving the sensibility of our pupils we only make them easier prey to the propagandist when he comes. For famished nature will be avenged and a hard heart is no infallible protection against a soft head. . . .

The little human animal will not at first have the right responses. It must be trained to feel pleasure, liking, disgust, and hatred at those things which are pleasant, likeable, disgusting, and hateful. . . .

And all the time—such is the tragi-comedy of our situation—we continue to clamour for those very qualities we are rendering impossible. You can hardly open a periodical without coming across the statement that what our civilization needs is more 'drive', or dynamism, or self-sacrifice, or 'creativity'. In a sort of ghastly simplicity we remove the organ and demand the function. We make men without chests and expect of them virtue and enterprise. We laugh at honour and are shocked to find traitors in our midst. We castrate and bid the geldings be fruitful.

The Abolition of Man, ch. 1

It must be remembered that in Mark's mind hardly one rag of noble thought, either Christian or Pagan, had a secure lodging. His education had been neither scientific nor classical—merely 'Modern'.

That Hideous Strength, ch. 9

What an answer, by the by, Wyvern [College] was to those who derive all the ills of society from economics. For money had nothing to do with its class system. It was not (thank Heaven) the boys with threadbare coats who became Punts, nor the boys with plenty of pocket-money who became Bloods. According to some theorists, therefore, it ought to have been entirely free from bourgeois vulgarities and iniquities. Yet I have never seen a community so competitive, so full of snobbery and flunkeyism, a ruling class so selfish and so class-conscious, or a proletariat so fawning, so lacking in all solidarity and sense of corporate honour.

Surprised by Joy, ch. 7

I have some difficulty in talking of the greatest things; it is the fault of our generation and of the English schools.

Letters (20 June 1918)

The very play
Of mind, I think, is birth-controlled to-day.
'To Roy Campbell', *Poems*

His education had had the curious effect of making things that he read and wrote more real to him than things he saw. Statistics about agricultural labourers were the substance; any real ditcher, ploughman, or farmer's boy, was the shadow Though he had never noticed it himself, he had a great reluctance, in his work, ever to use such words as 'man' or 'woman'. He preferred to write about 'vocational groups', 'elements', 'classes' and 'populations': for, in his own way, he believed as firmly as any mystic in the superior reality of the things that are not seen.

That Hideous Strength, ch. 4

Where the old education initiated, the new merely 'conditions'. The old dealt with its pupils as grown birds deal with young birds when they teach them to fly: the new deals with them more as the poultry-keeper deals with young birds—making them thus or thus for purposes of which the birds know nothing. In a word, the old was a kind of propagation—men transmitting manhood to men: the new is merely propaganda.

The Abolition of Man, ch. 1

'But do you really mean, Sir,' said Peter, 'that there could be other worlds—all over the place, just round the corner—like that?'

'Nothing is more probable,' said the Professor, taking off his spectacles and beginning to polish them, while he muttered to himself, 'I wonder what they *do* teach them at these schools.'

The Lion, the Witch and the Wardrobe, ch. 5

Speak about beauty, truth and goodness, or about a God who is simply the indwelling principle of these three, speak about a great spiritual force pervading all things, a common mind of which we are all parts, a pool of generalised spirituality to which we can all flow, and you will command friendly interest. But the temperature drops as soon as you mention a God who has purposes and performs a particular action, who does one thing and not another, a concrete, choosing, commanding, prohibiting God with a determinate character. People become embarrassed or angry. Such a conception seems to them primitive and crude and even irreverent. The popular 'religion' excludes miracles because it excludes the 'living God' of Christianity and believes instead in a kind of God who obviously would not do miracles, or indeed anything else.

Miracles, ch. 11

Liberal Christianity can only supply an ineffectual echo to the massive chorus of agreed and admitted unbelief. . . .

By the way, did you ever meet, or hear of, anyone who was

converted from scepticism to a 'liberal' or 'demythologised' Christianity? I think that when unbelievers come in at all, they come in a good deal further.

Letters to Malcolm, ch. 22

That structural position in the Church which the humblest Christian occupies is eternal and even cosmic. The Church will outlive the universe; in it the individual person will outlive the universe. Everything that is joined to the immortal Head will share His immortality. We hear little of this from the Christian pulpit to-day. What has come of our silence may be judged from the fact that recently addressing the Forces on this subject, I found that one of my audience regarded this doctrine as 'theosophical'. If we do not believe it let us be honest and relegate the Christian faith to museums. If we do, let us give up the pretence that it makes no difference. For this is the real answer to every excessive claim made by the collective. It is mortal; we shall live for ever. There will come a time when every culture, every institution, every nation, the human race, all biological life, is extinct, and every one of us is still alive. Immortality is promised to us, not to these generalities.

Transposition and Other Addresses, ch. 3

A great many of the ideas about God which are trotted out as novelties today, are simply the ones which real Theologians tried centuries ago and rejected. To believe in the popular religion of modern England is retrogression—like believing the earth is flat.

Mere Christianity, bk 4, ch. 1

Athanasius stood for the Trinitarian doctrine, 'whole and undefiled', when it looked as if all the civilised world was slipping back from Christianity into the religion of Arius— into one of those 'sensible' synthetic religions which are so strongly recommended to-day and which then as now, in-

cluded among their devotees many highly cultivated clergy-
men. It is his glory that he did not move with the times; it is
his reward that he now remains when those times, as all times
do, have moved away.

Introduction to *The Incarnation of the Word of God*,
by St Athanasius

4. THE ARTS

The pother about 'originality' all comes from the people who
have nothing to say; if they had, they'd be original without
noticing it.

Letters (*c.* August 1942)

I am afraid that some vainglorious writers may be encouraged to forget that they are called 'creative' only by a metaphor.
. . . All the 'creative' artists of the human race cannot so much
as summon up the phantasm of a single new primary colour
or a single new dimension. . . . Nor do artists give their so-
called creatures substantial existence.

Book review, *Theology* (October 1941)

Many modern novels, poems, and pictures, which we are
brow-beaten into 'appreciating', are not good work because
they are not *work* at all. They are mere puddles of spilled
sensibility or reflection. When an artist is in the strict sense
working, he of course takes into account the existing taste,
interests, and capacity of his audience. These, no less than the
language, the marble, or the paint, are part of his raw material;
to be used, tamed, sublimated, not ignored nor defied. Haughty
indifference to them is not genius nor integrity; it is laziness
and incompetence.

The World's Last Night, ch. 5

I think the only hope for poetry now lies in lowering [the poet's] status. Unless he speedily returns to the workmanlike humility of his great predecessors and submits to the necessity of interesting and pleasing as a preliminary to doing anything else, the art of poetry will disappear from among us altogether.

The Personal Heresy, ch. 5

When every one feels it natural to attempt the same kind of writing, that kind is in danger. Its characteristics are formalized. A stereotyped monotony, unnoticed by contemporaries but cruelly apparent to posterity, begins to pervade it.

The Allegory of Love, ch. 6, sec. 1

When grave persons express their fear that England is relapsing into Paganism, I am tempted to reply, 'Would that she were.' For I do not think it at all likely that we shall ever see Parliament opened by the slaughtering of a garlanded white bull in the House of Lords or Cabinet Ministers leaving sandwiches in Hyde Park as an offering for the Dryads. If such a state of affairs came about, then the Christian apologist would have something to work on. For a Pagan, as history shows, is a man eminently convertible to Christianity. He is, essentially, the pre-Christian, or sub-Christian, religious man. The post-Christian man of our own day differs from his as much as a *divorcée* differs from a virgin. The Christian and the Pagan have much more in common with one another than either has with the writers of the *New Statesman*; and those writers would of course agree with me.

'Is Theism Important? A Reply', *Socratic Digest* (1952)

Before leaving the Tree [Eve, in *Paradise Lost*] does 'low Reverence' before it 'as to the power that dwelt within', and thus completes the parallel between her fall and Satan's. She who thought it beneath her dignity to bow to Adam or to God, now worships a vegetable. She has at last become 'primitive' in the popular sense.

A Preface to 'Paradise Lost', ch. 18

It is a good rule, after reading a new book, never to allow yourself another new one till you have read an old one in between. If that is too much for you, you should at least read one old one to every three new ones. . . . Keep the clean sea breeze of the centuries blowing through your mind . . . by reading old books. Not, of course, that there is any magic about the past. People were no cleverer then than they are now; they made as many mistakes as we. But not the *same* mistakes. . . . Two heads are better than one, not because either is infallible, but because they are unlikely to go wrong in the same direction.

Introduction to *The Incarnation of the Word of God*, by St Athanasius

When the old poets made some virtue their theme they were not teaching but adoring, and what we take for the didactic is often the enchanted . . . that imaginary quarrel between the ethical and the poetic which moderns often unhappily read into the great poets . . . supposing that the poet was inculcating a rule when in fact he was enamoured of a perfection.

A Preface to 'Paradise Lost', Dedication

Admitted fantasy is precisely the kind of literature which never deceives at all. Children are not deceived by fairy-tales; they are often and gravely deceived by school-stories. Adults are not deceived by science-fiction; they can be deceived by the stories in the women's magazines. None of us are deceived by the *Odyssey*, the *Kalevala*, *Beowulf*, or Malory. The real danger lurks in sober-faced novels where all appears to be very probable but all is in fact contrived to put across some social or ethical or religious or anti-religious 'comment on life'.

An Experiment in Criticism, ch

The typical modern critic is usually a half-hearted materialist. He accepts, or thinks he accepts, that picture of the world which popularized science gives him.

The Personal Heresy, ch. 1

Of course the converted Intellectual is a characteristic figure of our times. But this phenomenon would be more hopeful if it had not occurred at a moment when the Intelligentsia (scientists apart) are losing all touch with, and all influence over, nearly the whole human race. Our most esteemed poets and critics are read by our most esteemed critics and poets (who don't usually like them much) and nobody else takes any notice. An increasing number of highly literate people simply ignore what the 'Highbrows' are doing. It says nothing to them. The Highbrows in return ignore or insult them. Conversions from the Intelligentsia are not therefore likely to be very widely influential. They may even raise a horrid suspicion that Christianity itself has become a part of the general 'Highbrow racket', has been adopted, like Surrealism and the pictures painted by chimpanzees, as one more method of 'shocking the bourgeois'.

'Revival or Decay?' *Punch* (9 July 1958)

It is perhaps worth emphasizing what may be called the hardness—at least the firmness—of Jane Austen's thought. . . . The great abstract nouns of the classical English moralists are unblushingly and uncompromisingly used: *good sense, courage, contentment, fortitude,* 'some duty neglected, some failing indulged', *impropriety, indelicacy, generous candour, blamable, distrust, just, humiliation, vanity, folly, ignorance, reason.* These are the concepts by which Jane Austen grasps the world. In her we still breathe the air of the *Rambler* and *Idler.* All is hard, clear, definable; by some modern standards, even naively so. The hardness is, of course, for oneself, not for one's neighbours

Contrasted with the world of modern fiction, Jane Austen's is at once less soft and less cruel.

'A Note on Jane Austen',
Essays in Criticism (October 1954)

That, perhaps, is where Scott differs most from the type of artist dear to the modern psychological critic. The blue devils do not haunt his work; they leave no trail of laudanum, drink, divorce, tantrums, perversions, or paranoia across his life.

They Asked for a Paper, ch. 5

[In Milton's time] men still believed that there really was such a person as Satan, and that he was a liar.

A Preface to 'Paradise Lost', ch. 13

Now the organisation of mass excitement seems to be almost the normal organ of political power. We live in an age of 'appeals', 'drives', and 'campaigns'. Our rulers have become like schoolmasters and are always demanding 'keenness'. And you notice that I am guilty of a slight archaism in calling them 'rulers'. 'Leaders' is the modern word. I have suggested elsewhere that this is a deeply significant change of vocabulary. Our demand upon them has changed no less than theirs on us. For of a ruler one asks justice, incorruption, diligence, perhaps clemency; of a leader, dash, initiative, and (I suppose) what people call 'magnetism' or 'personality'.

They Asked for a Paper, ch. 1

All men at times obey their vices: but it is when cruelty, envy, and lust of power appear as the commands of a great super-personal force that they can be exercised with self-approval. The first symptom is in language. When to 'kill' becomes to 'liquidate' the process has begun. The pseudo-scientific word disinfects the thing of blood and tears, or pity and shame, and mercy itself can be regarded as a sort of untidiness.

'A Reply to Professor Haldane',
Of Other Worlds

> If towering memory in our glance
> Reveals its pride, they call it names
> Like 'fantasy' or 'outworn romance'.
> So tireless propaganda tames
>
> All but the strong whose hearts they break,
> All but the few whose faith is whole.
> Stone walls cannot a prison make
> Half so secure as rigmarole.

'The Romantics', *The New English Weekly*
(16 January 1947)

The percentage of mere syntax masquerading as meaning may vary from something like 100 per cent. in political writers, journalists, psychologists, and economists, to something like forty per cent. in the writers of children's stories. . . . A good metaphysical library contains at once some of the most verbal, and some of the most significant literature in the world. . . . I doubt if we shall find more than a beggarly five per cent. of meaning in the pages of some celebrated 'tough minded' thinkers, and how the account of Kant or Spinoza stands, none knows but heaven. But open your Plato, and you will find yourself among the great creators of metaphor, and therefore among the masters of meaning.

Rehabilitations, ch. 7

Compare 'Our Father which art in Heaven' with 'The supreme being transcends space and time'. The first goes to pieces if you begin to apply the literal meaning to it. . . . The second falls into no such traps. On the other hand the first really *means* something, really represents a concrete experience in the minds of those who use it; the second is mere dexterous playing with counters, and once a man has learnt the rule he can go on that way for two volumes without really using the words to refer to any concrete fact at all.

Letters (17 January 1932)

The value we have given to that word ['Puritanism'] is one of the really solid triumphs of the last hundred years? By it we rescue annually thousands of humans from temperance, chastity, and sobriety of life.

The Screwtape Letters, ch. 10

The history of all arts tells the same miserable story of progressive specialization and impoverishment.

*Studies in Medieval and Renaissance
Literature*, ch. 4

If I have read the New Testament aright, it leaves no room for 'creativeness' even in a modified or metaphorical sense. Our whole destiny seems to lie in the opposite direction, in being as little as possible ourselves, in acquiring a fragrance that is not our own but borrowed, in becoming clean mirrors filled with the image of a face that is not ours. . . . An author should never conceive himself as bringing into existence beauty or wisdom which did not exist before, but simply and solely as trying to embody in terms of his own art some reflection of eternal Beauty and Wisdom. . . . And always, of every idea and of every method the Christian will ask not 'Is it mine?' but 'Is it good?'

'Christianity and Literature',
Christian Reflections

The patrons of sentimental poetry, bad novels, bad pictures, and merely catchy tunes are usually enjoying precisely what is there. And their enjoyment. . . . is not in any way comparable to the enjoyment that other people derive from good art.

It is tepid, trivial, marginal, habitual. It does not *trouble* them, nor haunt them. To call it, and a man's rapture in great tragedy or exquisite music, by the same name, enjoyment, is little more than a pun. I still maintain that what enraptures and transports is always good. . . .

The experiences offered by bad art are not of the same sort.
'Notes on the Way', *Time and Tide* (1 June 1946)

All that is not eternal is eternally out of date.
The Four Loves, ch. 6